GREECE: FROM RESISTANCE TO CIVIL WAR

GREECE:
From Resistance to Civil War

Edited by Marion Sarafis

Introduced by
Professor Nicos Svoronos

Spokesman

This book is copyright under the Berne Convention. All rights are reserved. Apart from any fair dealing for the purpose of private study, research, criticism or review, as permitted under the Copyright Act, 1956, no part of this publication may be reproduced, stored in a retrieval system, or transmitted, in any form or by any means, electronic, electrical, chemical, mechanical, optical, photocopying, recording or otherwise, without the prior permission of the copyright owner. Enquiries should be addressed to the publishers.

First published in 1980 by
Spokesman
Bertrand Russell House,
Gamble Street,
Nottingham

ISBN Paper: 85124 290 1
ISBN Cloth: 85124 289 8

Copyright © Society for Modern Greek Studies (ΕΛΕΜΕΠ)

Cover design: Eugenia Apostolou

Printed by the Russell Press Ltd., Bertrand Russell House,
Gamble Street, Nottingham

Contents

Editor's Foreword
Marion Sarafis.....................................7

Introduction
Professor Nicos Svoronos 9

*Greece in the Framework of Anglo-Soviet
    Relations 1941-1947*
Elisabeth Barker 15

*The British and the Greek Resistance Movements
    EAM and EDES*
Prokopis Papastratis 32

The Unnumbered Round
George Alexander 43

*The Mistakes of the Allies and the Mistakes
    of the Resistance*
Andreas Kedros..................................52

*EAM-ELAS: Resistance or National Liberation
    Movement?*
Thanasis Hajis 63

The Battle of Athens and the Role of the British
Heinz Richter 78

*The Don Stott Affair: Overtures for an
    Anglo-German local peace in Greece*
Hagen Fleischer.................................91

*The Russian Mission to the Greek mountains and entry
of EAM into the Government of National Unity*
Professor Nicholas Hammond (discussion only) 108

Panel Discussion 116

Appendix 134

Glossary and List of Contributors 136

Index. 138

Editor's Foreword

This book is an edited version of the proceedings of a conference held at the London School of Economics from 12th-13th May 1978. The conference was organised by the Society for Modern Greek Studies (ΕΛΕΜΕΠ) — an association of Greek academics and graduate students — together with the Union of Greek Univeristy Teachers and Research Staff in Western Europe.

In presenting these proceedings, the editor must first apologise to readers for two regrettable defects. For the loss of the first day's discussions on the papers by Elisabeth Barker, Prokopis Papastratis and George Alexander, due to breakdown of the tape-recorder, the organsers must bear responsibility. The absence of Professor Hammond's talk is in response to his own request. He has agreed however to publication of the fairly full subsequent discussion which gives some idea of the content of the talk. I would also like to take this opportunity of thanking him for his kindly encouragement which did much to overcome my initial hesitations about undertaking the work.

Many people have contributed to the production of this book which could more correctly be described as a collective effort. Richard Clogg, Lecturer in Modern Greek History, of King's College University of London, has throughout given the experienced advice so much needed by an inexperienced editor. There has been constant discussion with Roussos Koundouros of the Society's secretariat; Dr. Yanis Yanoulopoulos has been an ever-present help at all stages; Anna Syngelakis undertook the arduous task of transcribing the discussion tapes and has also acted as linguistic adviser for the Greek edition. In preparing both editions, with many of the contributors resident in Athens, Dr Prokopis Papastratis has proved an invaluable and most efficient "man on the spot" and has put in much work as my assistant in Greece. Finally, I would like to thank all the contributors for their interests and willing co-operation which has rendered the task of editing a real and a wholly unexpected pleasure.

The Conference organisers will, I am sure, join me in hoping that readers will find much that is new and much to interest them both in the stimulating papers and in the very lively discussion.

Marion Sarafis

Introduction

Resistance to the forces of fascism which began with the Albanian campaign (1940-41) continued throughout the years of Occupation and ended in civil war with its two phases (December 1944 — February 1945 and October 1946 — August 1949). This is the basic fact of the tragic history of Greece during that period.

Thus, the history of Greece presents a special aspect of a more general historical phenomenon which appeared with particular clarity during the Second World War: the genesis of mass popular resistance movements combining national liberation motives and aims directed against the foreign conqueror with motives and aims of a social and political character directed towards more or less radical internal change.

The distinguishing character of the Greek case is that one of the most widespread and deeply-rooted of the resistance movements in the countries of the Anti-fascist alliance ended in an armed clash between the forces of the left-wing EAM Resistance and the Greek Right which, with the support of the British armed forces, prevailed and, after the capitulation of the Left, imposed a climate of terrorism which led directly to the second phase of civil war and ultimately to the military dictatorship of 1967-74.

Naturally, written records of this tragic period of Greek history abound. But it is only in the most recent years that it has become the object of scientifically-based historical research. It is both the lapse of time and more particularly the opening of European and American official archives which have made this study possible.

The proceedings of the ΕΛΕΜΕΠ (Society for Modern Greek Studies) Resistance History conference contained in this volume are a contribution to that study. The papers were presented either by students of the period who have devoted considerable time and intellectual effort to academic research into the history of the Greek Resistance on the basis of original sources, or by participants who played a leading part in the events themselves. They are thus an exceptionally useful contribution to future study, more especially as they represent almost the complete range of conflicting opinions.

It is the assignment of responsibilities for the internal dissension leading eventually to armed conflict which is the theme of most of the papers.

George Alexander, taking up the position of Churchill which has been questioned by many researchers and by a large section of political opinion both in the US and in Britain, attempts a formalised assessment of KKE and ELAS political activity to prove that responsibility lay exclusively with ELAS and KKE who acted in accordance with a predetermined and well-organised plan for the seizure of power by force. It was a case of consistent conspiracy against the legitimate political representation of the Greek State as constituted by the King and the successive Greek monarchist governments, in the formation and composition of which the author does not perceive any British intervention.

For Andreas Kedros, responsibility must be divided between Churchill's personal policy and the policy of EAM. For him, Churchill's "mistakes" consist in over-estimation of the strategic importance of Greece for the imperial road to India and to oil; likewise in under-estimation of the "antipathy which Greeks feel towards a Russian-style Communism" for the imposition of which neither Greek psychology and mentality nor the "garden-produce" character of the Greek economy are suitable. Having wrongly assessed the aims of EAM-ELAS as the imposition of a communist regime on Greece, Churchill based his policy on support for the King who was responsible for the imposition of the Metaxas dictatorship on Greece. He did not fear to face the possibility of a conflict resulting from the imposition of his own policy and secured the consent of Roosevelt and Stalin who agreed on a Great Power policy of spheres of influence in complete opposition to the principle of national self-determination.

To Churchill's "mistakes" must be added the "mistakes" of EAM-ELAS, especially the inability of the leadership to adapt its strategy and tactics to the real balance of power. Thus, they lost control over the behaviour of certain sectarian elements towards the other Resistance organisations (EDES & EKKA) and a climate of civil war was created even before the December clash. The EAM leadership let itself be manoeuvred sometimes by Papandreou, sometimes by the Soviet Military Mission, sometimes by Churchill. These spasmodic oscillations resulted on the one hand in complete political capitulation and on the other in a failure to appreciate the capacity of the British forces to resist and the political will of Churchill to impose his policy on Greece. So the leadership accepted the armed challenge of December 1944, falling into a carefully laid trap.

Dr. Richter starts from the position that the December conflict was not the outcome of a planned revolution. KKE was not a threat to the social order. Faithful to the orthodox party doctrine which required the achievement of bourgeois democracy as a necessary pre-condition of any socialist programme, KKE looked with suspicion on some of the measures introduced by EAM-ELAS to speed up social change and reacted against these. The internal policy programmes of the left-wing organisations for the post-war period were based on a form of liberal democracy which should secure popular sovereignty and progress towards democratic social reform. Their foreign policy aimed at a real independence for Greece. This programme imperilled the Greek oligarchy. Churchill's intervention, in careful preparation since 1943 both at the diplomatic and the military levels, made it impossible to avoid armed conflict.

Thanasis Hajis gives his main emphasis to the internal factor and in particular to the strategy and tactics of the KKE leadership. For the former Secretary of EAM, the aims of that organisation were very different from those of the resistance organisations of Western Europe. This national liberation movement led the way to revolutionary changes in the direction of popular sovereignty which it was able to apply in part, in the mountains of Free Greece. EAM, which had been founded on the initiative of communist cadres, from the start raised the issue of power on the basis of the enormous majority of the Greek people whose support it had won and not as a result of the advance of the Soviet Army. The balance of power within Greece and also on the international plane made the policy of winning power a reality. The responsibility for defeat lies with the EAM leadership which lost heart and by ever-increasing concessions handed over power to Greek and foreign reaction. This course of action facilitated British intervention.

These interpretive essays, with their contrasting conclusions, are reinforced by the detailed research papers of Elisabeth Barker, Hagen Fleischer and Prokopis Papastratis who present a summary of the results of their investigations in the British and German archives, with much new material for the student.

Dr. Fleischer investigates the activities of the New Zealand officer Donald John Stott who, in collaboration with a Greek "Nationalist" right-wing movement and with the British authorities, tried to arrange an understanding between the German Occupation forces in Greece and the British. The main problem which he tries to solve is how far Stott's action formed part of a more general British policy or whether it was merely a case of private adventurism. If the evidence which the author has been able to collect is not such as to permit of a definite answer to this question, nevertheless it permits him to put forward the following hypothesis: Churchill may well have favoured the peaceful withdrawal of the Germans from Greece regarding this as conducive to the formation of a front to halt the advance of the Soviet Army into the Balkans. A certain correspondence of interests between Hitler and the British could mean that temporary, restricted local agreements of a tactical military character were not excluded.

British policy towards the Greek Resistance organisations is examined by Prokopis Papastratis who has organised and assessed the rich material to be found in British archives. The author traces the various phases of this policy: the failure of the attempt to bring EAM-ELAS under British control; the British turn towards EDES; the negotiations between the British authorities and the Greek monarchist governments and the forces of EAM, and their repercussions on the relations between the resistance organisations in Greece. This factual report brings out very clearly the general aims of British policy and its various gradations and even apparent contradictions at different stages and phases of its realisation. The author stresses the effort of British policy to overcome its basic contradiction: support for the monarchy and its governments which were regarded as a guarantee of exclusive British influence in Greece and the need to use the most important Greek resistance force, that of EAM-ELAS, for military operations with however the ultimate aim of preventing by every means its eventual acquisition of power.

This is the explanation of the "opposition" between the British military authorities with their short-term military aims and the British government which was pursuing a long-term policy.

After many vicissitudes, the various negotiations led to the Lebanon Agreement, to the entry of EAM into the Government of National Unity, then to the Caserta Agreement and the sending of British forces to Greece with the consent of the Greek authorities and with the implicit — or even explicit — agreement of the Soviet Union.

Elisabeth Barker gives us a detailed examination of Anglo-Soviet relations from 1941-47 and the course of negotiations between the two powers relative to the Balkans and especially to the Greek problem. The information she gives us from British official archives, especially from the Eden documents relating to his meetings with Stalin and other Soviet leaders, is particularly welcome to the historian and is one of the most important contributions presented in this volume.

Here we have the true "positions" of the Great Powers on matters of the uttermost importance to the Balkans and to Greece, naturally in the way that they were understood and presented from the British angle: the settlement of the frontiers of the Balkan states after the war, the problem of spheres of influence in that region are the main issues which occupy Great Britain and the Soviet Union. The author's detailed record, year by year, of the main points of these negotiations goes far to confirm and define the general impression from other western sources: the Greek problem does not seem to have been a focus of interest for Soviet policy. Not only from the well-known Moscow and Yalta Agreements, but from the first soundings taken by Eden in 1941 it already appeared that Soviet policy would find little difficulty in reaching an understanding with Great Britian on the Balkans, recognising British influence in Greece in exchange for British recognition of Soviet influence in the Northern Balkans. The historian must, of course, await the necessary confirmation from the Soviet archives, especially as regards the Soviet attitude to KKE policy and to the civil war.

All the papers presented here make a real contribution to the study of the Greek Resistance, either because they present, even in summary form, well-organised new material; or because each one of them presents particular aspects of a many-faceted subject. Thus, they stimulate thought and contribute to the widening and enrichment of the dialogue. Towards this end, I would like to add here a few thoughts of my own.

The Greek Resistance and its consequences are the turning-point of a much longer period of history which, for Greece, begins with the end of the First World War and the Asia Minor disaster of 1922.*

This is a period of fundamental economic, social & political change bringing with it the disarticulation of old structures and the appearance of new articulations marking the beginning of a new period of history.

The effects of this period of destruction and reconstruction and their direct and indirect consequences for the social and political life of Greece were naturally felt with intensity at a moment of general crisis such as the occupation of Greece by the fascist powers. The rhythm of change was quickened, consciousness of old contradictions extended to ever-widening spheres of Greek society, deepening perhaps at some points without this necessarily meaning that it contributed, in all the counter-balancing political forces, to the formulation of a clear ideological frame-work and to the crystallisation of a definite strategy and tactics for the realisation of an explicit social programme.

In spite of this, most studies relating to the period with which we are concerned — and those published here are in no sense an exception — even when they turn their attention to developments within the country, concentrate on the political aspect: the attitude of the parties to the war, and to the resistance; the resistance organisations and their relations with the political parties and amongst themselves, and this mainly in the sense of the determinant influence of one or other of the foreign powers active in Greece on the attitude of this or that Greek political organisation whose actions usually make it appear as a mere puppet of external agencies.

It is perhaps not superfluous to repeat here that such a line of thought can lead to the writing of studies presenting a series of important value judgements either justifying or condemning the policy of one or other party or resistance organisation or the policy of one or other of the foreign powers towards Greece. This perpetuates the old *syndrome* of Greek historiography, the *syndrome* of "the foreign hand" and of conspiracy in politics.

Of course, the significance of the external factor for the whole development of modern Greek history is a long and generally established fact and has repeatedly and rightly been stressed by Greek and foreign historians. And certainly in discussion of the Greek Resistance, analysis

---

* The defeat of the Greek campaign to liberate the Greek population of Asia Minor which resulted in the expulsion of that population with much loss of life and the flooding of Greece with refugees.

from the angle of foreign intervention seems particularly justified, not only because this is an inseparable component of the wider topic of the war fought by all the anti-fascist forces in which Great Britain, The Soviet Union and the United States played the major role; but also because the sources so far accessible for relevant study are sources outside Greece which naturally give most weight to the relations of these powers between themselves or with the Greek Resistance.

But we must not forget that within an analysis so angled may lurk a methodological error: the characterisation of foreign intervention as an autonomous historical factor and first principle of interpretation. The historian of this period must be fully conscious, especially when presenting interpretations, that thorough consideration of a phenomenon such as the Resistance can only be achieved on the basis of the history of developments within Greece, seen not simply as pre-conditions or as a fixed general framework within which events take place but as dynamic factors at every moment influencing the course of events and determining their complicated and ever-changing relations. And this holds equally for interventions from outside Greece; even if, at first sight, their weight appears to have a crushing effect on the development of Greek history.

The need for such a revision in the hierarchy of causes and for a change in outlook and viewpoint from which to consider the facts of the Resistance is urgent. And it is beginning to become possible, at least to a certain degree: on the one hand due to the continuing publication of a growing store of archive material and of various memoirs and testimonies from those who took an active part in events, as well as of studies each putting forward from its own viewpoint a particular aspect of Greek actuality; and on the other due to the multiplication in recent years of studies contributing to the analysis of modern Greek society and of the Greek economy.

Nicos Svoronos

Greece in the Framework of Anglo-Soviet Relations 1941-1947

Elisabeth Barker

I want to trace briefly the role of Greece in Anglo-Soviet relations during the Second World War and the immediate post-war period, basing myself almost entirely on the British official records. I would take as starting-point the brief and militarily unsuccessful British campaign in Greece in 1941. British motives for undertaking this campaign were too complex, both politically and psychologically, to be discussed here. More relevant is the consequence of this campaign for the British. In spite of the failure of their intervention in Greece, it left Churchill and Eden with a proprietary and protective attitude towards Greece. The sentimental and emotional element in this attitude should not be under-estimated; I myself should guess that in Churchill's mind it was almost as important as long-term considerations of British strategic interests as a Mediterranean power. As for Eden, he bore a considerable personal responsibility for the decision to undertake the Greek campaign; his political reputation at home suffered from its rapid collapse, and he was only human if he wished to justify the campaign, in retrospect, by establishing a permanent and especially close Anglo-Greek relationship. For Churchill, there was also the conviction that wherever the British had fought, there they also had certain special obligations and rights; and he had perhaps a certain tendency to inflate the number of British troops who fought and died in Greece.

At the time of the Greek campaign, the Soviet Union was very much on the margin of events. I do not think it possible to argue seriously — as has been attempted — that Churchill launched the campaign in order to delay Hitler's invasion of the Soviet Union, even though it may have had this effect. But in December 1941, when Britain and the Soviet Union were fighting together, Eden visited Moscow to discuss the possibility of an Anglo-Soviet treaty; and he then found himself faced by Stalin with a blue-print for post-war Europe, setting out Soviet interests. This did to some extent involve Greece. Stalin suggested that Yugoslavia should be restored and extended at the expense of Italy, but he said nothing about Macedonia or the Yugoslav-Greek frontier. Albania, Stalin said, might make an independent state with that independence guaranteed. (This was at a time when the British

Foreign Office did not dare to say anything about the independence of Albania for fear of offending the feelings of the Greek exiled government or Greeks at home). Turkey, Stalin said, should receive the Dodecanese; he added that islands in the Aegean especially important for Greece should go to Greece, but the Dodecanese should be returned to Turkey. Greece herself, Stalin added, should be restored in her old frontiers.

As for Bulgaria, Stalin said that the boundary between Turkey and Bulgaria should be adjusted so as to include in Turkey certain districts south of Bourgas populated by Turks, since Bulgaria ought to be punished for her attitude in the war. What was noteworthy here was that Stalin said nothing about giving Bulgaria an Aegean outlet. When in November 1940 the Soviet Assistant Foreign Minister, Sobolev, had visited Sofia in an effort to pre-empt Hitler's opening bid to persuade Bulgaria to sign the Tripartite Pact, he had, according to information reaching the British, specifically offered Bulgaria an Aegean outlet. A year later, therefore, Stalin had at least for the time being reversed this position. However, until the end of 1944 the British continued to suspect the Soviet Union of working for such an outcome.

It is perhaps worth noting the atmosphere of this conversation between Stalin and Eden in December 1941. In a discussion of the military situation, Eden said, 'What about the position of Turkey. Can we do anthing to improve that situation?' Stalin replied: 'Tell them they will get the Dodecanese.' Eden said: 'That is very difficult with the Greeks, as the islands are mostly inhabited by Greeks and the Greek people have long planned to have them.' Stalin said 'You cannot be very strict in pursuing this nationality principle. Also in Greece there are Turks.' Eden said: 'Do you think it would have an effect upon the Turks?' Stalin answered: 'All these islands blockade the outlet from Turkey. You could arrange an exchange of islands between Greece and Turkey so that some went to one and some to the other.' Eden then said' 'Some time ago when we thought we might take the Dodecanese we started conversations with Greece and Turkey, but they did not go at all well.' Stalin said 'The Turks would also like to have Dedeagatch, but we must not offend the Greeks, but I think there might be an exchange of islands.' Eden said, 'It is certainly worth exploring.' In further discussion of Turkey's role in the war, Eden said: 'As long as they remain a buttress against Germany they are a great help to us. Stalin answered: 'I think they must be paid for it.'[1]

These exchanges show that at least in talking to Eden Stalin was entirely pragmatic, non-ideological, un-Marxist or one might even say pre-Marxist, talking in terms of buying off potential allies, bribing potential allies, and dividing up the expected spoils of victory. Eden answered in the same spirit but did take some account of Greek feelings and claims.

One other point in these exchanges is worth noting. Stalin suggested that Britain might like to have bases at Boulogne and Dunkirk, perhaps also in Belgium and Holland and even in Norway and Denmark, as counterpart to the bases the Soviet Union wanted in Romania and Finland. But he did *not* suggest that the British might like bases in Greece. So it could perhaps be deduced that Stalin had a certain interest in Greece, though a negative one — that is, that he did not want to see the British permanently established there in the post-war world.

Eden could not however agree to Stalin's offer of bases in northwest Europe, or to the secret protocol Stalin had proposed, or to any commitment about post-war frontiers. Nor was there ever any formal war-time Anglo-Soviet agreement on Balkan frontiers. It was fixed British policy to make no such war-time commitments, in part because it would have caused deep offence to high-minded Americans. However, in the Anglo-Soviet treaty negotiations in the spring of 1942, Eden did offer to concede the Soviet-Romanian frontier of 1940, and, although this concession was not included in the treaty which eventually emerged from the negotiations, Eden continued to regard himself as bound by it; and this made it easier for him to contemplate the percentage agreement of 1944 which will be discussed later.

One further point about the Stalin-Eden talks was important. Eden advocated the formation of federations in east and south-east Europe. Stalin said: 'If certain of the countries wish to federate, then the Soviet Union will have no objection to such a course.'[2] This one sentence had a somewhat exaggerated long-term influence on British policy. At that time Greece and Yugoslavia were concluding an agreement which Eden hoped might be the nucleus of a future Balkan Union, to which Bulgaria and perhaps even Romania might eventually belong — a development which would of course have tended to preserve and safeguard their independence of the Soviet Union. But during 1942 Soviet diplomatic representatives let it be known that they disliked the idea of any federations which could be suspected of having an anti-Soviet tendency; and in spite of all assurances by Eden and others, they made it clear that they did have such suspicions. The Greek exiled government was very sensitive to Soviet signs of displeasure[3] and the Greek-Yugoslav agreement soon withered away. The British Foreign Office continued nevertheless to support the concept of Balkan and central European federations until finally at the Moscow conference of Foreign Ministers in October 1943, Molotov dealt it a death blow, and Eden buried it with his customary grace.[4] So this possible — but perhaps never really practicable — British-sponsored solution of the problem of relations between Greece and her Balkan neighbours vanished away, never to return.

Soviet suspicion of plans for Balkan union was not directed solely against the British. In the summer of 1943 the Yugoslav Partisan General Vukmanović-Tempo, Tito's representative in Yugoslav Macedonia, was busy establishing links with the EAM-ELAS in Greece and with the Albanian and Bulgarian Communist Partisans; he proposed that there should be a 'Balkan Staff' to coordinate their war effort and perhaps also their post-war efforts to prevent 'reaction' from enjoying the fruits of war. In August 1943, the Yugoslav Communist Party Central Committee vetoed Vukmanović-Tempo's initiative as politically incorrect and harmful. It seems likely that Moscow had a hand in this veto, but I have no evidence for this guess.

One other small incident over Greece's relations with her neighbours is worth noting. In December 1941, Stalin had told Eden that Albania should be independent. In January 1942 Eden told the Soviet ambassador in London that he shared Stalin's view but that in view of Greek and Yugoslav claims on Albania he was not anxious to commit himself for the time being.[5] In November 1942 however the British Special Operations Executive — SOE — were anxious to stimulate resistance in Albania, and prodded by them, the Foreign Office again considered the matter, and finally told the Soviet and US governments that they intended to make a declaration on Albanian independence, inviting them to do the same. Both Moscow and Washington agreed. But when the British told the Greek exiled government of their intention, a government crisis resulted. In consequence the British delayed publishing the declaration until 17 December, and added to it a specific pledge that Albania's frontiers would have to be settled at the peace conference. The next day the Soviet Foreign Ministry issued a much more enthusiastic statement which made no reservations about Albania's frontiers.

It was during 1942 that SOE developed their contacts with EAM-ELAS which soon led to friction between SOE and the Foreign Office, and, in time, to bitter complaints from King George II and the Greek exiled government. But the British Foreign Office do not at this time seem to have believed or suspected that EAM had any contacts with the Soviet Union, (as they did in the case of Yugoslavia). They continued to act as though Greece was a special British responsibility or preserve. Even during 1943, the British continued to talk as though they could, if necessary, clash openly with EAM-ELAS or try to break with them, without any repercussion on Anglo-Soviet relations.

All the same, in the latter part of 1943 the threat of a Communist Greece in the post-war world began to be a nightmare haunting Churchill and Eden. Following the crisis of August 1943 which followed the abortive visit to Cairo of the six resistance leaders from Greece, including Communists, the South African Prime Minister, General Smuts — who was deeply respected by Churchill and who took a close personal interest in Greek affairs — sent Churchill a personal and most secret message urging him to support the King's return to Greece in advance of any plebiscite. Smuts wrote: 'I very much fear that in the inflamed condition of public feeling not only in Greece but also in other Balkan countries, chaos may ensue after the Allied occupation unless a strong hand is kept on the local situation. With politics let loose among those people we may have a wave of disorder and wholesale communism set going all over those parts of Europe. This may even be the danger in Italy, but certainly in Greece and the Balkans.' Reading this message from Smuts, Eden wrote to Churchill that he agreed with much of it and thought the matter should be discussed with Roosevelt (this was at the time of the first Anglo-American Quebec conference). After consulting Roosevelt, Churchill sent George II a message: 'We are all looking forward to your returning to Greece at the head of your armies and remaining until the will of the Greek people is expressed under conditions of tranquillity.' Roosevelt approved Churchill's move and agreed to send a parallel message to the king, though, as Churchill put it, 'his angle as head of a republican government is not necessarily identical with ours but there is no difference in aim'.[6]

At no point did Churchill, Eden or Roosevelt consider consulting Stalin on this question; and at this stage, the Soviet government seemed outwardly entirely passive in Greek affairs. During the autumn of 1943 there was a crisis in relations between the British and EAM-ELAS owing to ELAS's actions against rival resistance groups. At the Foreign Ministers' conference in Moscow towards the end of October, Eden gave a somewhat bland and smooth account of the situation, telling Molotov that in Greece a number of British officers were active in blowing up railways and carrying out other destruction; shelter had been given to them by a number of guerrilla bands with whom they had been living for some time. Large areas of the country were not under German control at all. Some months ago, Eden went on, British officers had obtained agreement between all the guerrilla bands; recently this agreement had broken down but, he went on, 'we are going to try and patch it up again, because if they fought each other sabotage work would not be facilitated.' To judge by the British record, Molotov does not seem to have made any objection to British policy in Greece.[7]

Eden also submitted to the conference a draft declaration providing for joint three-power responsibility for Europe as a whole, as against 'separate areas of responsibility' (or what might also have been called "spheres of influence"). But Motolov said he thought it superfluous; the Soviet government had never expressed the idea of 'separate areas', so why bother to refute it? Eden said he wanted to reassure the smaller powers, but nevertheless agreed to leave the proposals over for the next conference.[8]

If Molotov had accepted the British prosposal for joint three-power responsibility in Europe, Eden would have been obliged from then on to consult the Soviet Union over Greece. As Molotov rejected it, he did not. Immediately after the Moscow conference Eden went to Cairo and found himself embroiled in a heated argument between the British ambassador to the Greek exiled government, Reginald Leeper, and the

British Commanders-in-Chief in the Middle East, over the right way to handle the crisis in relations with ELAS. When he got back to London, Eden reported to the War Cabinet on 14 November, and argued that the political disadvantages of continuing support to EAM outweighed the military advantages to be expected from continued support. In his report he wrote: 'Pro-British sentiment in Greece is strong and universal, but... our support of the king is unpopular... The Russians showed no interest at the Moscow conference in the Greek situation, and it may be that they regard Greece as being within our sphere of influence: but this attitude might well change if EAM gained complete control of Greece.'[9] So Eden seemed to be arguing that British action to *prevent* EAM from taking power would be the best way of *stopping* the Soviet Union from interesting itself in Greece. The argument might sound nonsensical, but may have contained more sense than appeared on the surface.

After long and inconclusive discussion of the Greek problem in the War Cabinet Eden reported to Churchill — who was at that moment on his way to Cairo *en route* for Teheran — that he himself had argued that continued British support for EAM would mean 'assisting a gang of extremists whose aim is to seize control of Greece against the wishes of the majority of the Greek people', and that 'under EAM rule Greece would look to Russia and not to ourselves for support.'[10] So the solution, Eden claimed, was to discredit the Communist leaders and detach the non-communist rank and file from them; if this was to be done, George II must be persuaded to declare that he would not return to Greece until the people had declared their will, and meanwhile he should nominate a regency council which, when the moment came, was to be set up by Archbishop Damaskinos of Athens.[11] Churchill, however, replied that this made him grieve deeply and he preferred to wait until Eden arrived in Cairo before approaching the king.

On 22 November 1943 the War Cabinet again discussed the matter. A Minister — the minutes do not state which — asked whether the Soviet government should be informed before the British took action which might result in the Germans being able to withdraw some forces from Greece. Eden again said that at Moscow he had mentioned the matter to Molotov who had shown no interest and said that he regarded it as a British affair. The War Cabinet then authorised Churchill and Eden to handle the question in consultation with the British military authorities in the Middle East.[12]

As things turned out, it was not until *after* the Teheran conference that Churchill and Eden, in Cairo, were able to tackle the matter. Churchill, most unhappily, agreed to Eden's request that he should say the final word which would persuade George II to take the necessary action. Before Churchill could actually do so, Roosevelt, for reasons which are still obscure, strongly advised the king to stand firm and not to give way to the British — in particular, to Eden. General

Smuts, also in Cairo, gave the king the same advice. The whole plan for a public declaration by the king, and arrangements for a regency council, fell to the ground, possibly to Churchill's personal satisfaction, certainly to Eden's great annoyance and frustration.

The result was that top-level British policy towards EAM remained unsettled and uncertain in the opening months of 1944. Churchill became more and more violent in his dislike of EAM-ELAS; the British military leaders urged the necessity for holding down German divisions in the Balkans and retaining links with EAM-ELAS for this purpose; Eden continued to press for the Damaskinos solution.[13] On 24 February Churchill approved Colonel Christopher Woodhouse's efforts to bring about agreement between EAM-ELAS and Colonel Zervas, but said that if these failed a British commander-in-chief of the guerillas should be appointed. On 29 February Colonel Woodhouse secured agreement between ELAS, Zervas and EKKA, using the threat of public denunciation to achieve this. [14]

While all this was going on the Soviet Union continued — so far as the British were aware — to stand aloof. But in April 1944 — a crucial month in Anglo-Soviet relations — the situation changed. Partly because of the establishment in the Greek mountains of the PEEA — a higher political organ of EAM-ELAS with an obvious potential claim to the status of a provisional Greek government — and partly, too because of the continued stubborn refusal of George II to make any political gesture, disorders, developing into mutiny, broke out in the Greek armed forces in the Middle East. Eden, physically exhausted, was sent on sick leave, and Churchill, with considerable glee, took over as acting Foreign Secretary. He took an especial interest in quelling the Greek mutinies with an ostentatiously firm hand.

In mid-April the situation was darkened by what the Foreign Office interpreted as deliberate Soviet intervention in the Greek troubles in the Middle East. On 15 April the Permanent Under-Secretary, Sir Alexander Cadogan, drew Churchill's attention to a message from Cairo from the Soviet news Agency, Tass, strongly critical of the Greek exiled government and, as Cadogan put it, by implication of the British government's action also. This report had been published in all Soviet papers and used in Soviet broadcasts to Greece, and had been followed by a further Tass message on the same lines. Leeper, the ambassador, had suggested a strong protest in Moscow. Cadogan wrote to Churchill: 'In the past the Russians have shown only a limited interest in Greece and I had hoped that they would continue to let us handle Greek affairs as we see fit; but these Tass messages show that they are now apparently determined to intervene. The line they are taking is most unhelpful and is bound to undermine the effect of our own action since the lack of unanimity between ourselves and the Russians is clear for all to see.' Cadogan urged Churchill to complain to Moscow.[15]

Churchill replied that he had been very much annoyed by the Tass messages but thought the trouble could have been avoided if the Russians had been kept informed. He then sent Molotov a long message, in part drafted by the Foreign Office. His own personal words were: 'I hope the Tass Agency will not make our task more difficult than it is. This is really no time for ideological warfare. I am determined to put down the mutiny... I am sure you would not allow such things to go on in the Soviet armies or among any forces which you might control. I therefore hope that Tass may be told to leave off this agitation in which they are engaged, the only result of which may well lead to bloodshed which I hope to avoid.[16]

Churchill's message to Molotov was sent off on 16 April. On 22 April Molotov replied. The Soviet government, he wrote, had so far extremely limited information on the Greek question; the British government, which had its military mission in Greece, was in a more favourable position. He would therefore be grateful for additional information on Greek affairs. Tass, Molotov added, could not bear any kind of responsibility for the shedding of blood, but had been instructed to verify its information more strictly. After this more or less conciliatory reply on Greece, Molotov turned to Romania, with which tentative peace negotiations were in progress, and wrote: 'now it is for us to increase from all sides the pressure on the Romanians so that they shall abandon their hopeless and criminal position.'[17] Molotov seemed thereby to be making a link between Greece and Romania.

Three days later Churchill sent Molotov a confident message on the Greek mutinies saying that both the naval mutineers and the mutinous brigade had surrendered, with no Greek casualties.[18] Molotov replied with a message dated 28 April, which was read over the telephone to Churchill at his country home on 30 April. This was decidedly less friendly. Molotov wrote that the latest changes in the Greek government hardly signified that a stable situation had been reached or that the legitimate desires of those Greeks who were the representatives of the Greek national movement had been taken into consideration. From Churchill's words, Molotov went on, it was clear that the British government controlled Greek affairs and the Greek government 'in the most direct manner'; Churchill should therefore understand that the Soviet government could not accept any responsibility for Greek affairs or for the British government's measures. Molotov then once again turned to Romania, complaining coldly that Churchill had not yet said what steps the British government intended to take with regard to greater pressure on the Romanians, as desired by the Soviet government.[19]

So far, Churchill had been determined to keep control of Greek affairs firmly in British hands, while informing the US and the Soviet Union — after the event — of what he had been doing. When on 12 April he had heard that a suggestion had been made in Cairo that the American and Soviet ambassadors to Greece should jointly state that the American and Soviet governments were in complete agreement with the British, he sent a telegram to Leeper: 'On no account accept any assistance from American or Russian sources otherwise than as specially enjoined by me.'[20] Thereafter he accepted with pleasure a curious message from Roosevelt to the Greeks which could be taken to support British policy. But he made no move to secure any such Soviet message. All he wanted, it seemed was that the Russians should keep out of Greek affairs.

At the beginning of May, Churchill became more and more worried that the Russians were definitely intending to intervene in Greece. These worries were linked with shock and indignation over sudden accusations by Molotov that the British were double-crossing the Soviet Union over Romanian affairs. These were conveyed in a harshly-worded message which Churchill received late on 30 April about a British party parachuted into Romania four months earlier, which had been immediately captured by the Romanian authorities and subsequently used, with the full knowledge of the Soviet government, as a channel of communication with both the Romanian government and the Romanian opposition leaders. Molotov had never before objected to this British mission, but now did so in terms which implied an accusation of deliberate British bad faith.[21]

The British ambassador in Moscow, Clark Kerr, immediately linked this Soviet display of suspicion over Romania with the Russians' 'apparent nascent tendency to play an independent hand in relation to Greece.'[22]

On the following day, 3 May, Leeper reported from Cairo that the Soviet representative in Italy had been trying to find out from the Greek representative about the British mission in Greece, and about its members; the Greek representative got the impression that the Russians were preparing to send a mission of their own to EAM and were trying to find a precedent by which this could reasonably be justified. Reading this, Churchill commented to Eden: 'We ought to watch this. We lost 40,000 men in Greece.'[23]

Eden was by this time back at work, and was trying to de-fuse some of the high tension in Anglo-Soviet relations which had built up during his absence. On 4 May Churchill sent him two minutes about differences with the Soviet government, putting the question, 'Are we going to acquiesce in the communisation of the Balkans and perhaps of Italy?. . . If our conclusion is that we resist communist infusion and invasion, we should put it to them pretty plainly.' He also suggested recalling the ambassador from Moscow: 'evidently we are approaching a showdown with the Russians.'[24]

A showdown was not what Eden wanted. On 4 May he saw the Greek ambassador who was worried about supposed Soviet intriguing with Greek Communists against Papandreou, the man whom the British now wanted to head a new Greek government representing all parties; the Greek ambassador asked if the British could not get the

Soviet government to help them in Greece, or at least refrain from hindering them. Eden said he hoped to discuss things with the Soviet ambassador.[25]

The next day, 5 May, Eden saw the Soviet ambassador, Gusev, and had what seems from the British record to have been a friendly talk on Romania and Greece. Eden started by saying that no more British missions would be sent to Romania for the time being and in any case the Russians would always be consulted; he added that Britain, as he had often said, thought that the Soviet Union 'should take the lead in our joint efforts to get Romania out of the war'. Then, turning to Greece, Eden said he was gravely concerned and there was a danger that Britain and the Soviet Union would diverge. Britain was backing Papandreou, a good democrat and a republican who wanted to bring all parties, including the Communists, into a broad-based government. He would like the Soviet government to support him publicly; if not, the Russians might at least tell the Greeks privately that it was EAM's duty to join Papandreou's government. Greece, Eden went on, was in the British theatre of command, so he felt entitled to ask for Soviet help there, just as the British gave help to the Russians in Romania, which was in the Soviet sphere of command.[26]

From the British record, it seems clear that there was nothing dramatic in Eden's proposal which was intended mainly to get over the difficulty of persuading EAM to enter the Papandreou government. Eden must almost certainly have discussed his move with Churchill in advance, though I have found no record of this. What is clear is that he did not think it necessary to mention it to the War Cabinet until after Gusev had responded. This Gusev did on 18 May, telling Eden that the Soviet government agreed to his suggestion, but that before giving any final assurance, they wanted to know whether he had consulted the US government. Eden said he did not think the Americans had been consulted but he could not imagine they would dissent. On the same day Eden informed the War Cabinet, again saying that he was sure there would be no difficulty with the Americans.[27]

Eden's confidence on this point was surprising, but Churchill seems to have shared it. On the same day, 18 May, Churchill wrote a long message to Roosevelt in which he said in passing: 'Although Molotov was most insulting about Romania, they have today told us they accept the broad principle that they take the lead in the Romanian business and give us the lead in Greece. I am quite content with this. A portent of the Soviet policy is to be found in the gushing message which I have received from the representatives of EAM now gathered, with all other Greek parties, in the Lebanon.'[28]

Churchill then apparently forgot that he had sent this bit of news to Roosevelt, who in any case seems to have taken no notice of it. (It has to be remembered that the launching of "Overlord" was only a week or two ahead). However on 21 May Churchill wrote to Eden that he would like to telegraph to Roosevelt about the arrangement with Gusev: 'He would like the idea especially as we should keep in close touch with him'. But the Foreign Office already had misgivings about the arrangement, commenting on 23 May: 'it is the thin end of the wedge towards spheres of influence.' Prompted by Churchill's minute to Eden on 24 May May, the Foreign Office sent an explanatory telegram to Washington, stressing that the British had 'no desire to carve up the Balkans into spheres of influence', and the proposal was just 'a useful device for preventing any divergence of policy' in the area.

The American State Department, in particular the Secretary of State, Cordell Hull, reacted most unfavourably, as the Foreign Office had feared, all the more since they had not been consulted in advance. On 10 June Roosevelt himself sent Churchill a very chilly message saying that such an arrangement would certainly result in the division of the Balkan region into spheres of influence despite the declared intention to limit the arrangement to military matters. Churchill, very much irritated, replied pleading for a three months' trial of the arrangement. Roosevelt at first agreed but then on 22 June more or less retracted his agreement, accusing the British of concealing things from the Americans. Churchill replied with some passion, saying he thought that Roosevelt had agreed that the Russians, the only power that could do anything in Romania, should direct things there; the Greek burden, he went on, 'rests almost entirely upon us and has done so since we lost 40,000 men in a vain endeavour to help them in 1941. . It would be quite easy for me, on the general principle of slithering to the left, which is so popular in foreign policy, to let things rip, when the King of Greece would probably be forced to abdicate and EAM would work a reign of terror.' Churchill said he could not admit he had done anything wrong. Four days later, Roosevelt finally agreed to a three months' trial.[29]

By this time over eight weeks had elapsed since Eden first put his proposal to the Soviet ambassador, so the Soviet decision to involve the Americans had enabled them to avoid committing themselves and to keep their hands free. During all this time, the EAM leaders in Greece were still refusing to allow their representatives to join the Papandreou government, as had been agreed at the Lebanon conference in May. Even after Roosevelt had agreed to the British proposal for a three months' trial, the Soviet government were not yet ready to bind themselves, and wanted to delay matters still further. On 1 July Gusev told Eden that since the Americans had 'some apprehensions' about the proposed arrangement, the Soviet Union must make a direct approach to Washington. On 12 July Churchill sent Stalin a message urging the need for at least a three months' trial as agreed by Roosevelt: 'These may be three very important months, Marshal Stalin, July, August and September,' Churchill wrote.[30] On 15 July the State Department addressed a memorandum to the Soviet government giving grudging consent to the three months' trial, but adding that the US government had apprehensions about the division of the Balkans into spheres of influence, and hoped that no projected measures would be allowed to prejudice efforts for allied collaboration rather than independent action, since any arrangement suggestive of spheres of influence could only militate against the establishment of a broader system of general security (in other words, the projected United Nations Organisation which was Cordell Hull's favourite child).[31]

Seeing this, Churchill minuted to Eden on 1 August: 'Does this mean that the Americans have agreed to the three months' trial, or is it all thrown into the pool again?' Eden replied that it seemed to mean the the Americans would agree to the trial period but would much prefer that the Russians should turn the whole scheme down. Eden added: 'As for the Soviet government's attitude, the unheralded despatch of their mission to ELAS speaks for itself. I have as you know taken this up strongly with Gusev. . . If the Russian reply is at all conciliatory there might still be a chance of getting them to recognise our predominant position in Greece, but otherwise I fear not.'[32]

The British had in fact been unpleasantly surprised, even shocked by the arrival of the Soviet mission. Eight officers, after misleading the British as to their intentions, had flown from Bari, in Italy, to a SOE landing ground in ELAS territory in northern Greece on the night of 25 to 26 July. Eden commented on this news: 'On the face of it this may be a Russian attempt to complete Communist domination of the Balkans and I think we should make it pretty plain that we are not standing for it in Greece.' The British Chiefs of Staff estimated that this 'attempt by the Russians to build up EAM means that probably 80,000 rather than 10,000 British troops would have to be sent to Greece.'[33]

In the long term this estimate was not far out. In the short term the arrival of the Soviet mission to EAM did not have the effects Eden had feared. A few days after its leader, Colonel Grigory Popov, had visited the PEEA, this body, which had been holding out strongly for seven seats in the Papandreou Government, suddenly agreed to be content with five seats. The Papandreou Government of National Unity was finally formed on 2 September. In Moscow, however, Molotov brushed off British complaints about the unexpected arrival of the mission, telling the British ambassador that there was no Soviet-British agreement on prior consultation and no agreement about Greece.[34]

On 23 August King Michael of Romania carried out an anti-German coup which opened the way for the Red Army into Bulgaria and thereafter into Yugoslavia and Hungary. The whole military position in south-east Europe was transformed, very much to the advantage of the Soviet Union. The British were afraid that the Russians would back up the Bulgarians in holding on to Greek territory and claiming the permanent outlet on the Aegean promised by the Russians in November 1940. They also became increasingly afraid — with some justification —

of joint Yugoslav-Bulgarian claims for the inclusion of Greek territory in an autonomous Macedonia. On 17 September Eden — then in Quebec — telegraphed to the Foreign Office about the possibility of recognising that the Soviet Union should take the lead in Bulgaria 'provided that they recognise that HMG should take the lead in Greece. . . We would have to be assured that the Soviet Union recognises the predominant position of HMG in all arrangements for Greece now and after the actual state of war has ended.'[35]

So by this time, in Eden's mind, all idea of a three months' trial period had faded away; he was planning for a post-war world. But the first British task was to instal the Papandreou government in Greece, with the support of a very small British force, which was all that could be spared, and in the face of potential opposition from EAM-ELAS, in spite of the agreement of the ELAS commander to place all forces under the British General Ronald Scobie. On 21 September the British ambassador in Moscow, under instructions, said that a British force was about to be sent to Greece and recalled Britain's special interest in Greece, expressing the hope that the Soviet government would not find it necessary to send Russian troops into any part of Greece except in agreement with the British. Two days later, rather surprisingly, Vyshinski said that the Soviet government 'confirmed' the 'agreement' of May 1944 about theatres of operation and had no intention of sending forces into Greece.

In early October, Churchill and Eden arrived in Moscow. Roosevelt was preoccupied with the coming American presidential election — but still wanted to stop Churchill making any deal with Stalin in which he was not involved — or which he might find difficult to explain to the American voters. Churchill, however, seeing the hard facts of Soviet military predominance in south-east Europe, felt it urgent to save what could be saved from the empire which he believed Stalin to be building, and which was rapidly taking shape. He was in fact determined to do a deal, even if it meant going behind the back of his friend Roosevelt.

Stalin, on his side, seemed to want to encourage Churchill in this direction. At their first meeting, on 9 October, the American Ambassador, Averell Harriman, who had been instructed by Roosevelt to observe the Anglo-Soviet discussions, was excluded. Churchill told Stalin that, while he would welcome Harriman at a number of their talks, he did not want this to prevent 'intimate talk' between Stalin and himself. Stalin said Roosevelt seemed to be demanding too many rights for the US, leaving too little for the Soviet Union and Britain, who after all had their treaty. Churchill then said that he was not worrying very much about Romania. That was very much a Russian affair. But Greece was different. Britain, he said, must be the leading Mediterranean power and he hoped Stalin would let him have the first say about Greece in the same way as Stalin about Romania. He then produced what he called a 'naughty document' showing the relative interests of the Soviet Union and 'the others' as 90 to 10 in Romania, and 10 to 90 in Greece, with less extreme figures for Bulgaria, Hungary and Yugoslavia. The Americans, Churchill said, would be shocked if they saw how crudely he had put it, but Stalin was a realist, he himself was not sentimental and Eden was what he jokingly called 'a bad man'. Churchill added that he had not consulted the British cabinet or parliament.[36]

Stalin, so Churchill wrote later, ticked the paper after a slight pause. There was later wrangling about the percentages for Bulgaria, Hungary and Yugoslavia, but the percentages for Greece and Romania were not questioned by either side.

Once he had done this deal with Stalin, in the shape of this percentage agreement, Churchill then got cold feet and felt uneasy and unhappy about it, and its possible effect both in Britain and the US; it was therefore kept strictly secret; Roosevelt only got an innocuous version of it. But when the Soviet Union refrained from public intervention in the civil war which broke out in Greece in December 1944, Churchill was to some extent comforted. Nevertheless, if the Soviet press abstained from criticizing the British, the press of Greece's northern neighbours, Yugoslavia and Bulgaria, took a strongly pro-EAM and, at least by implication, anti-British line. There were also reports of material aid to ELAS with Soviet blessing over the Yugoslav and Bulgarian borders. In Athens, when Papandreou's Foreign Minister, Dragoumis, sent a representative to call on Colonel Popov at the Russian Embassy on 8 December, Popov expressed great sympathy for EAM and for ELAS with whom, he said, he had shared the hardships of mountain warfare for five months. Popov also said that the major part of the Greek people sided with EAM and expressed regret that innocent women and children were being killed.[37] Popov was also reported to have been seen going round photographing in areas where fighting was going on, so embarrassing the British forces.[38] But the British did not take Popov's activities seriously. On 16 December Eden instructed the ambassador in Moscow to express to Molotov his appreciation of the Soviet government's attitude as shown in the restraint of the Soviet press.[39]

Nevertheless, the Soviet attitude remained extremely reserved and unclear. In March 1945 Sophianopoulos, the Foreign Minister, told Leeper that he had been informed that a Soviet ambassador would not be sent to Greece, and he thought that the Soviet authorities did not intend to appoint one until Greek Communists entered the government; he said criticism of the government was increasing in the Soviet press.[40]

Churchill, once he had made his dramatic Christmas flight to Athens and approved Damaskinos, thereafter presiding over the first meeting between Damaskinos and the EAM representatives, seems to have been quite genuinely anxious to get out of the Greek entanglement as quickly as possible. He wrote to Eden on 7 January 1945 that British policy in Greece should be purely military, namely to hold the Attica region long enough for Damaskinos's government to set up a military force to keep order, after which British troops should be withdrawn at the earliest moment. 'I should say,' Churchill wrote, 'that four months was the utmost limit for any British troops to stay in Greece. I hope they may be very rapidly reduced before then.' Again in April 1945 he wrote to Eden: 'We are still aiming steadily at the old bull's eye viz a free, unfettered plebiscite as between monarchy and republic and free unfettered elections. . . This might take place in three or four months and when we are in a position to persuade the Greek government to offer front seats to British, Russian and American representatives.'[41]

But Stalin had no intention of sending Soviet observers to watch Greek elections, any more than he wanted British and American official observers at Bulgarian or Romanian elections. In practice, because of continuing unrest and disorders in Greece, the first post-war elections were not held until March 1946 and were then watched by the Allied Mission for Observing the Greek Elections – which contained no Russians.

By this time the Greek Communist Party was headed by Nikos Zachariadis, who had been found by Allied troops at Dachau and flown back to Greece in an RAF aircraft in May 1945. The Party's popularity had suffered by the removal of hostages from the Athens area after the fighting of December 1944, and also from the widespread belief that it was in league with the Communist armies to the north who wanted to annex Greek territory. To counter this second embarrassment, EAM backed the government's claims for the annexation of Albanian and Bulgarian territory. However, as Zachariadis explained when I interviewed him in 1946, this was a tactical move to appease the non-Communist groups allied with the Communists in EAM; the Party's real policy was that the northern frontier questions should be settled on the basis of self-determination. As for possible Yugoslav claims, Zachariadis said that territorial questions between Greece and Yugoslavia did not arise. The population of Greek Macedonia was 90% Greek and only 10% Slav and EAM stood for the territorial integrity of Greece.

The policy of the Communist Party in the 1946 election was to boycott them utterly under the slogan "*Apoche*" (Abstention). It could perhaps be regarded as a success for the Communists that only 60% of potential voters actually voted; but the practical result was a victory for the combined royalist groups. So the royalist, Tsaldaris, came to power and in the following September there was a further vote in favour of George II's return to Greece. There then followed the third round of the Greek civil war.

In spite of this the Foreign Secretary, Ernest Bevin, proposed to the British cabinet in January 1947 that British forces in Greece should be reduced by 1 April to one brigade of four battalions, which would remain in Greece only until the withdrawal of Soviet forces from Bulgaria, 90 days after the ratification of the Bulgarian peace treaty which was to be signed in February. At the same time Bevin told the Cabinet that as regards long term military or economic aid to Greece, the US should be asked what part of the burden they would bear.

So began the British withdrawal from Greece and American intervention in Greek affairs, heralded by the announcement of the Truman Doctrine on 12 March 1947. On this, it is perhaps worth quoting Bevin's comment: The Soviet government, he said, had overplayed their hand in Greece and by making the British task too difficult and costly, had provoked US intervention.[42]

To sum up, I think it is fair to say that if Stalin, for tactical reasons, was willing to let the British establish a military presence in Greece in 1944, from 1945 onwards he tried, in a rather uncertain and spasmodic way, to get them out again. The British were in fact forced to leave, not by Soviet pressure, but by their own grave financial and economic difficulties, and they did not leave until they were confident the Americans would take their place. In this sense Stalin's policy was self-defeating. As for British policy during these years, it brought no material gain to Britain. But I personally believe that it procured for the Greeks a wider freedom of choice — though freedom of choice is always limited for small countries — than they would have had otherwise.

Footnotes: All the following are source references to documents in the Public Record Office in London which are quoted by permission of the Controller of H.M. Stationery Office.

1. FO 371/3284 WP (42)8
2. Ibid.
3. FO 371/33133 Eden despatch R 974/43/67 10.2.42
4. FO 371/37031 N 6921/5412/G
5. FO 371/33107 Eden despatch to Cripps R 332/G 13.1.42
6. PREM 3 211/4 S. Africa (HC) 1100 20.8.43; Eden minute 22.8.43; WELFARE 490 31.8.43; WELFARE No. – 13.9.43.
7. FO 371/37031 Record of Proceedings of the Foreign Ministers' conference N 6921/541
8. FO 371/37031 Record of 12th meeting 30.10.43
9. PREM 3 211/7 WP(43)518 14.11.43
10. PREM 3 211/6 GRAND 102 19.11.43
11. Ibid.
12. CAB 65/40 WM(43)160 C.A. 22.11.43
13. PREM 3 211/9 Eden minute PM/44/61 10.2.44, Churchill minute M 76/4 6.2.44

14. PREM 3 211/9 AFHQ 2454 5.3.44
15. PREM 3 211/16 Cadogan minute PM/44/248 15.4.44
16. PREM 3 211/16 Churchill addition to FO draft message to Molotov 16.4.44
17. PREM 3 211/16 Molotov message T.913/4 2.4.44
18. PREM 3 211/16 PM Message T.953/4 25.4.44
19. PREM 3 211/16 Molotov message T.1004/4 28.4.44
20. PREM 3 211/11 PM's telegram T.908/4 14.4.44
21. FO 371/43999 FO 1310 to Moscow 30.4.44
22. FO 371/43999 Moscow 1142 2.5.44
23. PREM 3 211/16 Cairo (Leeper) 299 3.5.44; Churchill minute 7.5.44
24. FO 371/43636 Churchill minutes M.497/4, M.498/4 4.5.44
25. FO 954/11 (280)
26. FO 371/44000 Eden despatch R7214/9/G 5.5.44
27. FO 371/43636 FO 1560 to Moscow 25.5.44, WM(44) 65 18.5.44
28. PREM 3 472 PM to President 678 T.1095/4 19.5.44
29. FO 371/43636 PM to President 712 T.1342/4 23.6.44; PREM 3 66/7 President to PM 570 T.1364 27.6.44
30. FO 371/43636 Gusev letter to Eden 30.6.44, FO 2079 to Moscow 12.7.44
31. FO 371/43636 Washington 4028 25.7.44
32. FO 371/43636 Churchill minute M.912/4 1.8.44, Eden minute PM/44/578 8.8.44
33. FO 371/43772 Eden minute 3.8.44; COS(44)257(0) 3.8.44 Ismay minute 3.8.44
34. FO 371/43772 Moscow 2206 21.8.44
35. PREM 3 79/1 GUNFIRE 247 17.9.44
36. FO 800/302 Record of meeting at Kremlin 9.10.44, first draft
37. FO 371/48294 Chancery letter 2.1.45
38. FO 371/43772 Athens 560 11.12.44
39. FO 371/43699 FO 4735 to Moscow 16.12.44
40. FO 371/48294 Athens 690 6.3.45
41. FO 954/11 Churchill minutes M.29/5 1.7.45, M.314/5 8.4.45
42. FO 371/66368 Moscow 965 24.4.47

The British and the Greek Resistance Movements EAM and EDES

Prokopis Papastratis

The subject of this paper is British relations with the Greek resistance movements EAM and EDES. Based mainly on the Foreign Office documents, it attempts to examine British policy towards these resistance movements and how it was achieved in the general context of the Anglo-Greek relations during this period.

The battle of Greece ended at the end of May 1941 when Crete was occupied by the Germans. The King and his hastily formed Government left Crete for the Middle East first and then for London. In Greece a political void was created as a result of the collapse of the Metaxas regime and the departure of the King and his Government. The leaders of the old political parties were unwilling and unable to fill it as they were cut off and had no influence upon the Greek people, while at the same time they were opportunistically hesitant to cooperate with the Greek Government in exile. This political void was filled by EAM-ELAS which expressed the will of the Greek people to resist the enemy. EAM was formed in September 1941 and ELAS in April 1942. The old political leadership with the exception of Canellopoulos showed a negative attitude on the issue of the resistance while the Tsouderos Government remained non-committal if not indifferent. EAM-ELAS was a rapidly expanding popular and political mass resistance movement where KKE was predominant and which was independent of the traditional political parties, of the Greek Government in exile and of the British. EAM-ELAS was not the only resistance movement but it soon become the more important one. The British reaction to the formation of EAM-ELAS is not yet known because the relevant documents are still not available. There is no doubt however, that in the summer of 1942 and especially after the arrival of Canellopoulos and Colonal Bakirjis in the Middle East the British authorities were sufficiently informed about EAM's character. During this time SOE was in contact with a group of republican officers who were planning to form guerrilla bands in the mountains but were hesitant to take the final decision.[1] The decision therefore of EAM to form ELAS and start guerrilla activities no doubt made SOE put pressure on these officers to put their plans into practice, but without success. Thus, from these republican officers, only Zervas, who along with Pyromaglou had formed EDES, was willing to take up arms. EDES' political complexion was socialist but it lacked a consistent ideology. Zervas however was reluctant to leave Athens for the mountains in spite of the strong pressure exerted upon him, He finally did so under the threat that he would be exposed to the Germans.[2] It is obvious that for the British Zervas was the only alternative solution to an EAM monopoly of the resistance and this must be the reason why they kept the pressure on him, although he was considered as disreputable by the British authorities in Cairo.[3] The other alternative resistance organisation to EAM-ELAS was EKKA which also had a socialist political complexion. EKKA however was too slow to take the field and when it did so in the spring of 1943, in the area of Amfissa, EAM-ELAS was already strongly established there. In the summer of 1942 it became apparent to the British that EAM-ELAS did not depend for its attitudes and policy on them, in contradistinction to EDES and the Tsouderos Government. Consequently it was realised that their policy of support for the King and his Government was contradictory to any support for and cooperation with EAM-ELAS. Nevertheless due to the importance of the resistance for the Allied war effort, attempts were made to bridge this basic contradiction by trying to reorganise the whole resistance movement in such a way as to be coordinated and controlled by the British authorities in Cairo. These attempts were made by the Anglo-Greek Committee in Cairo through the Tsigantes mission and the six Colonels in Athens. These attempts failed to materialise, the main reason being that EAM-ELAS was an already established resistance movement which could not be ignored or forced to submit itself to this reorganisation. As a result the only alternative solution for the British to the expansion of EAM-ELAS was to support EDES and EKKA. In the meantime and quite independently of these efforts taking place in Athens, a British military mission had been established in the mountains under Brigadier Myers after his group, along with ELAS and EDES forces, had blown up the Gorgopotamos bridge late in November 1942.

This failure to control the resistance movement from Cairo coincided in March 1943 with the deterioration of the relations between the Foreign Office and SOE over the issue of policy to be followed regarding Greece. This was a typical case of conflict between short-term military objectives and long-term political interests. The Foreign Office maintained that SOE by supporting EAM-ELAS for guerrilla activities was practically building up an opposition to the King and his Government whom the British Government had pledged to support. Therefore the Foreign Office tried to curb SOE activities in Greece but the Chiefs' of Staff opinion to the contrary prevailed. The result of this interdepartmental conflict was the despatch of contradictory instructions to the British military mission in Greece. Thus the British liaison officers were instructed that their mission remain a merely military one and that they should at all times avoid getting involved in political discussions. They were also instructed that the British Government's wish was that they should not ever hesitate to show their confidence in the King and Government.[4]

In the meantime in Greece, Myers had developed in early February 1943 the idea of forming "National Bands". These bands would be non-political, militarily unified and under the command of the Commander-in-Chief Middle East. SOE had agreed to give the maximum support to them and when these bands would be sufficiently strong ELAS would be invited to join them. Colonels Zervas, Psarros and Sarafis, the latter at that time with an independent band in Thessaly, agreed to this plan.[5] It is clear that the scheme aimed at minimizing the political activity of the guerrilla bands and as such it was concerned with the political activity of ELAS. For this reason Myers, having realised that EDES under Zervas would not present any problems in this respect, wished to strengthen the National Bands first and then invite ELAS to join them. What Myers and Woodhouse had in mind was a network of independent National Bands throughout the country, with British liaison officers passing on the instructions from the General Headquarters Middle East and acting as arbitrators in disputes. With this pattern ELAS would have to conform in order to continue receiving supplies. But EAM realised that the British had quite different intentions for the guerrilla movement from their own. The question involved, put briefly, was whether the resistance would consist of small, basically British-controlled guerrilla bands or of a large EAM-controlled popular army. Consequently, EAM counterproposed in their draft agreement the establishment of a Joint General Headquarters, responsible directly to the C-in-C Middle East with powers to settle disputes, send bands from one area to another and appoint military commanders.[6] Cairo and London did not accept the EAM draft agreement because, as they pointed out to Myers, it was designed to bring all bands under EAM's control as this organisation would dominate the Joint General Headquarters. Myers was also told that the struggle for control of the bands was a symptom of something more fundamental: this was the aim of EAM to seize power and realise their political ambitions as opposed to the policy of the British Government which was to support the King and his Government. On the other hand the Foreign Office did not accept Leeper's repeated proposal for a showdown with EAM. In this they were probably influenced by an SOE memorandum on the possibilities of splitting ELAS from EAM. This paper exposed the difficulties of such a course of action, pointing out that it could not be done without political help. The Foreign Office however, believed that a successful showdown with EAM at that time would be desirable in order to avoid it later when British troops would land in Greece. But they doubted whether this showdown would be successful as in the ensuing civil war they would have to support EDES against EAM which was at the time the most powerful organsiation in Greece. As a result it was decided that the negotiations with EAM should continue while at the same time a distinction should be drawn between the political leaders of EAM and the rank and file and that all the fire should be concentrated upon the former. At the end the British accepted the two most important EAM proposals, namely that there should be a Joint General Headquarters responsible directly to the C-in-C Middle East and that the British liaison officers should not have any authority to issue orders but limit their functions to liaison. Final agreement was reached in early summer of 1943.[7] This was indeed a modification in the Foreign Office attitude towards EAM. It can be explained by the fact that the Foreign Office realised that no other policy could be adopted towards EAM at the time. The British acceptance of EAM's proposals in the Military Agreement was clearly the result of military necessity, as EAM-ELAS was indispensable for the operation "Animals" which aimed at distracting German attention from the landing in Sicily.

The basic problem facing the British Government regarding the Greek political situation was whether EAM would attempt to seize power at the time of liberation. The Foreign Office expected that the Anglo-American invasion of the Balkans, under consideration at the time, would solve this problem. But the success of this operation was bound to be affected by the strong popular opposition to the King. At this point the British policy of support for the King became openly contradictory. On the one hand the Foreign Office decided that the King should declare that he would submit the question of the regime to a plebiscite, to prove that the British would not impose him on an unwilling people with their bayonets; on the other Churchill as well as the Foreign Office decided that in spite of the War Office objections the King should return to Greece with the first British troops.[8] This contradiction was due to the fact that the Foreign Office wished to appeal to the moderates, as it used to call them. At the same time the Foreign Office was prepared to use the King as a rallying point in its effort to prevent EAM from gaining political predominance in Greece at the time of liberation. The unpopularity of the King and its consequences for British policy was a permanent feature which the Foreign Office had to face during all this period. Furthermore it is characteristic that the intervention of Churchill, the basic supporter of the King, in the Greek political situation increased from the time the opposition to the King became increasingly confirmed.

In autumn 1943 the fact that no Allied operations would take place in the Balkans brought the question of an EAM coup to seize power to the forefront. This question was actually presented in a more acute form as reports from Greece confirmed the reinforcement of EAM's position and the fact that the King's return would be actively opposed.

As a result British policy, without abandoning its basic principle of support for the King, was readjusted according to the existing political and military situation. Therefore the British Government accepted Leeper's proposals which amounted to the following: to break with EAM and attempt to divide it by discrediting its leadership and winning over its moderate members; the King to pledge that he would not return to Greece until the question of the regime had been settled and to appoint Archbishop Damaskinos as Regent. The last proposal was in fact a tactical withdrawal to an earlier demand by the opposition including EAM to the King, which the British Government had turned down a few months earlier. The question of the plebiscite had also been raised by Myers earlier in 1943 but the Foreign Office had turned it down with indignation. This proposal however, as it was combined with a rupture with EAM, was meant to help in winning the moderates from EAM and uniting them under Damaskinos. The refusal of the King — unexpectedly reinforced by Roosevelt — to give this pledge and appoint Damaskinos as Regent removed from this policy the arguments which would render it appealing to moderate opinion and help to undermine the unity of EAM-ELAS. As a result this policy of directly attacking the EAM leadership was abandoned. In fact it was partially implemented, because the decision already in force to stop sending supplies to EAM-ELAS due to the civil war was reaffirmed.[9]

On 9 October 1943 civil war broke out in central and western Greece between ELAS and EDES which lasted until the end of January 1944. On the receipt of this news Cairo ordered the suspension of supplies to both sides. But, as evidence from British liaison officers showed that ELAS was the aggressor, the supplies to Zervas were soon resumed and in fact increased, as Cairo feared that he might be annihilated by ELAS. ELAS had the initiative in this phase of the civil war but the supplies sent to Zervas enabled him to hold his own. During the period of the civil war Zervas and ELAS received the following supplies (October 1943 to January 1944 inclusive)[10]:

Food and clothing:	Zervas 14 tons	ELAS 34 tons
Arms and ammunition:	Zervas 74 tons	ELAS 22 tons
Gold Sovereigns:	Zervas 18,000 coins	ELAS 927 coins

Out of the 22 tons sent to ELAS the first 16 were sent to them from October to mid-November 1943 to carry out special operations only, as approved by the Middle East Defence Committee. But in early November Churchill ruled that 'EAM and ELAS should be starved and struck by every means in our power'.[11] As a result, only 6 tons were sent to ELAS with the approval of MEDC, but this time for special operations in Eastern Macedonia, away from the scene of civil war. Out of the 74 tons sent to Zervas, 50 were received during December, while the January sorties to him were limited because more aeroplanes were not available.

EKKA which remained neutral in the civil war received in this period 14 tons of ammunition, 3,600 gold sovereigns and 2 tons of food and clothing.

On 20 December 1943 Woodhouse reported from Greece that ELAS as well as EDES had indicated their readiness to consider proposals to end the civil war. But on 4 January 1944 the civil war flared up again as Zervas attacked ELAS forces under Aris Velouchiotis. During the previous December Colonel Barnes, the Senior Liaison Officer with Zervas, had twice encouraged him in this sense. On 11 December Barnes had reported to Cairo. 'Zervas realised he must smash the ELAS soon to be of use to us, which I tell him is our reason for supporting him.'[12]

Two days later Zervas had received a stricture from GHQ Middle East regarding his not attacking the Germans and had expressed his willingness to do so. Barnes reported to Cairo: 'I told him I did not consider him strong enough to attack both ELAS and the Germans simultaneously, and preferred him first to consolidate himself as there would soon be plenty of action against the Germans. He has plans to clear Jumerka of ELAS very soon.'[13]

But although Barnes definitely encouraged Zervas to undertake this attack, it has not yet been ascertained whether Barnes himself was instructed in this sense by Cairo as a large number of documents bearing on these events remain closed. However the Foreign Office had informed Leeper on 4 November 1943 that it was established that Zervas should be given full liberty, in consultation with Barnes, to take what action he considered necessary for his defence.[14] Thus when Barnes reported that Zervas would obey Middle East orders implicitly and that he could "stop him fighting ELAS with a word" Cairo was of the opinion that: 'It is not thought desirable to order him to desist until either EAM have agreed to the principle of reconciliation or until Zervas has attained his immediate objective, the occupation of all Epirus.'[15]

Woodhouse was also of the same opinion and he telegraphed to Barnes from his Headquarters: 'We are pleased as you are, about Epirus developments. ELAS General Headquarters are rattled and increasingly friendly to me. I believe now there is a good chance of settlement. Almost all extremists and fanatics have been conspicuously absent during the last few weeks. I presume you can stop Zervas crossing the Akheloos River. I should be delighted to see him here, but I doubt if it would help.'[16]

It is clear from the relevant documents that the British authorities viewed the Zervas successes in the civil war as a means to strike a balance between Zervas and ELAS and to strengthen Zervas' position in the resistance movement.

As Woodhouse pointed out, in a report on the civil war he sent to SOE Cairo in October 1943, EAM-ELAS had since last March been too strong for the Allied Military Mission to enforce a policy upon them. He also stressed that the probable outcome of the civil war would be an increased strength in the hold of EAM-ELAS on Greece.[17] The civil war stopped early in February 1944 in order to allow the negotiations for settlement to begin, but only after ELAS had counter-attacked and had driven Zervas' forces back to the point from which they had started.

It is quite possible that Zervas would have reacted the way he did in the civil war irrespective of Colonel Barnes' encouragement. Zervas was strongly anti-communist and, as Woodhouse had reported late in September 1943, he had a strong royalist following in his organisation. Woodhouse also reported after the civil war had started that by that time a great many undesirables used EDES as an asylum to escape from EAM-ELAS and had turned it into a general refuge from EAM. This fact, added Woodhouse, was probably welcomed by Zervas.[18]

EAM's participation in the civil war would be explained by the fact that it no doubt wanted to have the monopoly of the resistance and at the same time was afraid of any efforts to undermine its position. In the negotiations which followed the civil war the aims of EAM and the British were completely contradictory. EAM wished to settle the issue of the formation of a single national Government and then discuss military matters such as the formation of the united army. On the contrary, Woodhouse pointed out to Cairo that the success of the ELAS plan to neutralize Zervas' bands depended on the achievement of the National Government as proposed by EAM. Therefore military problems should be settled before a coalition Government was created. Cairo agreed and additionaly instructed Woodhouse to achieve a geographical demarcation of the areas to be controlled by Zervas and ELAS.[19]

At the conference which followed at Plaka[20] in February 1944 the three main resistance organisations EAM-ELAS, EDES and EKKA were represented. But soon Kartalis, the EKKA representative and chairman of the conference, expressed to Woodhouse his strong feelings against EAM-ELAS and told him that his sympathies were wholly with EDES and that EKKA would back no solution unless EDES agreed. As for Pyromaglou and Zervas, they kept asking Woodhouse for precise guidance all the time.[21] In fact, in the conference it was the British who were negotiating with EAM-ELAS and not Zervas or EKKA. It is therefore not surprising that the very next day after the conference had started Woodhouse telegraphed that the negotiations had reached deadlock in practice but that they would continue in theory. Thus, the conference continued to meet because neither the British nor EAM wished it to break up. After several meetings no results were reached on the two subjects under discussion, the formation of a "Preparatory Government Committee" and the powers of a single Commander-in-Chief for the guerrillas. Woodhouse informed Cairo that the resumption of civil war was imminent. Cairo then authorised him to warn all concerned that in the event of civil war breaking out they would publicly denounce the leaders whom they considered to be at fault. Thus according to the British, ELAS agreed under pressure to sign a resolution, already accepted by Zervas and EKKA, to the effect that movements of guerrilla bands into each other's territory in case of operational necessity should not be regarded as hostile acts justifying resumption of civil war. Zervas and ELAS also agreed not to move into the other's territory beyond the line held by them on the eve of the truce. Leeper commenting on the signed agreement pointed out that the conference, which EAM had tried hard to make political, had concluded — due to Woodhouse's ability — with purely military decisions. And this was exactly what the British wanted.[22] In fact EAM had failed in their effort to form a National Government according to their terms. This led EAM to form PEEA, the Political Committee of National Liberation. The formation of PEEA worked as a catalyst in Greek affairs in the Middle East. The Greek Armed Forces revolted in favour of PEEA and, as a result of the crisis which followed, Tsouderos' Government resigned. This crisis was viewed by the British in the context of their policy towards EAM. This policy as it was formulated by Leeper aimed at the formation of a National Government where all the traditional political parties would participate united against EAM and where EAM would be invited to participate too. If EAM did decide to participate it would actually reduce itself to a minority party in it. At the same time the British obviously hoped that this decision would make it difficult, if not impossible, for EAM to seize power at the time of liberation. In case EAM refused to participate, the Foreign Office was prepared to denounce it to the Greek people and hold it responsible for breaching the national unity. Therefore what the Foreign Office needed was an able politician with a strong personality who would abide faithfully by the British policy and whom the British would confidently promote as the right person for the premiership of the National Government. In Papandreou they found a suitable prime minister for the occasion. Papandreou, the leader of a small splinter group of the old Venizelist party, was already known to the British for his anti-communism and was not involved until then in any of the numerous political intrigues. In the existing situation he was the only politician available to be used and as Eden pointed out, their only hope as far as he could see.[23]

The refusal of EAM to enter the National Government despite its initial agreement in Lebanon did not prompt the Foreign Office to break with this organisation.[24] The Foreign Office realised that only EAM's entry into the Government would secure the political stability in the Greek situation which was indispensable for the unopposed arrival of the British forces and the National Government in Greece.

The attitude of EAM regarding the issue of the National Government and its eventual participation in it still remains one of the most controversial questions of that period; the more so as no satisfactory explanation was ever given for this decision by the leadership of that organisation. The EAM decision to participate in the Lebanon Conference and even send a PEEA delegation was clearly contradictory to the formation of PEEA itself. This contradiction was apparently due to the difficulty of EAM and in fact of KKE, the leading political force in this organisation, in implementing its policy. There are two possible explanations for this difficulty of EAM: either it doubted whether it had the power to fulfill its policy or, and most probably, it had not clarified its own ideological conceptions as regards the existing political situation. EAM's decision to enter the National Government was the last of a series of policy revisions, not as yet adequately explained, which resulted in tactical defeats. In this decision the leadership of EAM and KKE were no doubt influenced by the fact that the Soviet Union had not recognised PEEA. They were also influenced by the Soviet advice available to them through Novikov and Popov.

The entry of EAM into the National Government secured for the British the political aspect of the Greek question. The military aspect of this question was secured with the despatch of a small British force to Greece with the approval of the Soviet Government and in accordance with the Caserta Agreement. The despatch of a British Force was viewed as a political necessity by the Foreign Office and Churchill on the one hand and as a military one by the Chiefs of Staff on the other. The Foreign Office view finally prevailed at the War Cabinet but not before Eden had stated that, unless a government friendly to Britain was established in Greece with the help of British forces, British political influence in S.E. Europe and its strategic position in the E. Mediterranean would be at risk. The importance attached by the Foreign Office to the despatch of British forces is clearly shown by their decision to prevent the early return of the King, in order to make the arrival of the British troops more acceptable. The Soviet Government did not hesitate in September 1944 to agree to the despatch of the British forces to Greece adding that it did not intend to send any Soviet troops there.[25] This Soviet decision was no doubt in accordance with the secret agreement on the Balkans which was *de facto* in force from the summer of the same year. With the Caserta Agreement the British secured the all-important Athens areas as well as control of the ELAS forces at the crucial time of liberation. EAM by signing this agreement was consistent in the policy it was following from the time it entered the National Government.

British policy towards Greece in the period under examination would have remained the same irrespective of the appearance or not of EAM. The creation of EAM and its influence resulted in British policy intervening much more directly than would have been necessary otherwise. The British used Zervas to the limit, in order to counter-balance the influence of EAM and they were successful to a certain degree.

They could not achieve more in the circumstances because Zervas' personality was self-defeating for this purpose. However the British policy was proved to be successful having achieved its initial aim, namely to restore its political influence in Greece.

Footnotes
1. K. Pyromaglou, *G. Kartalis*, Athens 1965, pp.154, 157-158. C.M. Woodhouse, Early British Contacts with the Greek Resistance in 1942, *Balkan Studies*, Vol.12, No.2, Thessaloniki 1971, p.362.
2. Woodhouse, *The Struggle for Greece 1941-1949*, London 1976, p.29.
   Woodhouse, Early British Contacts with the Greek Resistance in 1942, *Op.Cit.* p.358.
   Woodhouse, Summer 1943: the Critical Months, in *British Policy towards Wartime Resistance in Yugoslavia and Greece*, edited by Ph. Auty and R. Clogg, London 1975, p.119.
3. R7640 FO 371/33163 Warner to Dixon November 2, 1942.
4. R2050 FO 371/37201 "Political Aspects of the Greek Resistance Movement", March 6; minutes by Dixon March 7, 1943.
   R2133 FO 371/37216 Extract from War Cabinet Conclusions 38(43) March 8, 1943.
   R2363 FO 371/37222 "Policy towards Greece" FO Memorandum March 15, 1943.
   R2432 FO 371/37195 C.D. to Sargent March 16, 1943.
   R2434 FO 371/37195 General Ismay to Sargent March 17, 1943
   Ll. Woodward, *British Foreign Policy in the Second World War*, London 1971, vol.III, p.361.
   Woodhouse, Summer 1943 in Auty and Clogg, *Op.Cit.* p.137.
5. E.C.W. Myers, *Greek Entanglement*, London 1955, pp.114-116.
6. R4502 FO 371/37202 Sweet-Escott to Dixon, May 25, 1943; Texts of the two draft Agreements.
   Woodhouse, Summer 1943 in Auty and Clogg, *Op.Cit.* pp.123-124.
7. R4502 FO 371/37202 Cairo to Myers telegram 0765 May 27, 1943.
   R4697 FO 371/37202 Leeper to FO telegram 107 May 27;
   FO to Leeper telegrams 63 and 66 May 28, 31; minutes by Dixon May 29, 1943.
   R4753 FO 371/37202 Leeper to FO telegram 109 May 30, 1943.
   R4622 FO 371/37202 SOE Cairo, Memorandum "Possibilities of splitting the ELAS from EAM" May 12, 1943.
8. R4717 FO 371/37202 FO to Leeper telegrams 81 and 82, June 14, 1943.
   R5683 FO 371/37222 Major Holmes (WO) to Dixon June 28, 1943, R5684 FO 371/37222 C.D. to Sargent and Glenconner Memorandum June 28, 1943.
   R5586 FO 371/37222 Dixon Minute June 29, 1943.
9. R9703 FO 371/37231 Leeper to FO telegram 295 October 5, 1943.
   R10450 FO 371/37206 Archbishop Damaskinos to Minister of State, undated.
   WP (43) 526 "Policy towards Greece" Eden Memorandum Nov.21, 1943.
   WM (43) 160 Conclusions, Confidential Annex November 22, 1943.
   R12837 FO 371/37231 Eden to Churchill December 5,6 and 8; Churchill to Eden December 9; Leeper to FO telegram 379, December 7, 1943.
   CAB 65/40 WM 169 (43) 2 Confidential Annex December 13, 1943.
10. R2766, R2767 FO 371/43679 Leeper to FO telegrams 116 and 117 February 20, 1944.
11. R11098 FO 371/37207 Minute by the Prime Minister Nov.3, 1943.

12. R13508 FO 371/37210 Barnes to Cairo December 11, 1943.
13. R13769 FO 371/37210 Barnes to Cairo December 12, 1943.
14. R11098 FO 371/37207 FO to Leeper telegram 241 Nov. 4, 1943.
15. R544 R1046 FO 371/43676 Barnes to Cairo January 8 1944 and "Periodical Intelligence Summary No.2 up to 9th January 1944".
16. R544 FO 371/43676 Woodhouse to Cairo for repetition to Barnes January 10, 1944.
17. R11673 FO 371/37207 Col. The Hon. C.M. Woodhouse to Brigadier Keble "Recent Crisis in Free Greece" Pertouli, 19 October 1943.
18. Ibid.
19. R2260, R3222 FO 371/43678 Woodhouse to Cairo February 4 and 9, 1944.
20. In the Public Record Office files the Foreign Office designates what is usually known as the Plaka Conference by the name Merokovo, the popular name of the village of Myrofyllo, where the first stage of the conference took place.
21. R3430 FO 371/43681 Woodhouse to Cairo February 22, 1944.
    R3103 FO 371/43680 "Minutes of the 7th Meeting" February 21, 1944.
    R2846 FO 371/43679 Woodhouse to Cairo, February 15, 1944.
22. R3430 FO 371/43681 Woodhouse to Cairo February 28, 29, 1944.
    R3251, R3303, FO 371/43680 Leeper to FO telegrams 129, 132 February 28, 29, 1944.
    R3962 FO 371/43682 Woodhouse to Cairo March 1, 2, 1944.
23. R13126, R13188 FO 371/37209 Leeper to FO and FO to Washington telegrams 387 and 8714 December 12 and 17, 1944.
    R8897 FO 371/43688 Leeper to Eden May 24, 1944.
    R7081 FO 371/43702 Eden minute April 30, 1944.
24. R11504 FO 371/43714 COS Minute 1238/4 to Churchill July 19 and FO minutes July 24-28, 1944.
25. R12457 FO 371/43715, WO (44) 433 "Despatch of British Forces to Greece" Eden Memorandum August 8, 1944.
    R15250 FO 371/43747 Eden to Churchill PM/44/622 Sept. 27, 1944.
    R15679 FO 371/43777 Churchill to Eden M918/4 Sept. 29, 1944.
    R15193 FO 371/43692 Kerr to FO telegram 2530 Sept. 23, 1944.

The Unnumbered Round
George Alexander

During the Second World War there were two, evident bids by the Communist Party of Greece for control of its country. They are known as the "First" and "Second" Rounds, and were remarkably similar. Both featured an effort by the Communist Party to secure a position of dominance over the Greek State either by negotiation, or by force through the military strength of ELAS.

Take, for instance, the First Round, of the autumn and winter of 1943. Current in the Greek political world during the summer of 1943 was the expectation that the Germans were very soon to evacuate the Balkans. The prospect of an early liberation prompted the KKE openly to stake their claim to power in the Greece which was to follow the war. And the Communists desired complete power, which at first they attempted to secure by negotiation. During August 1943, the emissaries of EAM-ELAS who visited Cairo, the seat of the Greek Government-in-Exile, to negotiate with the bourgeois emigrés who constituted that Government's Cabinet, demanded that the resistance forces receive no less than the Ministry of the Interior, the Ministry of Justice, and the Ministry of Defence.

That constitutes complete power. For if I hold the Ministry of the Interior, my police arrest you. If I hold the Ministry of Justice, my courts try and imprison you; and if I hold the Ministry of Defence, should you escape, my troops will hunt you down.

The negotiations of August 1943 collapsed; there had never been a chance of success. Compromise is the stuff of which negotiations are made, but the Communists' demands were anything but conciliatory, and the bourgeois parties were not prepared to capitulate. Bullets, then, were substituted for words, as ELAS marched against EDES, the foremost armed threat to EAM. But for the surprisingly dogged resistance offered by EDES, by New Year's Day of 1944 **EAM-ELAS** might have been the sole substantial resistance organisation in Greece.

The Second Round, as is well known, was constituted by the protracted and painful negotiations between EAM and George Papandreou, Premier of the Government of National Unity, over the issue of demobilisation of the guerrilla forces. Here, too, one perceives a determined effort by the Communist Party to attain a dominant position within the State apparatus. When negotiations failed to produce results, the Athens ELAS — the 1st ELAS Army Corps — went over to the offensive.

The desire for complete power, and the pursuit of it by means of negotiation or, if need be, by force: where one discerns these elements, one recognises an attempt by the KKE to achieve control of Greece. On this basis, one can identify another "round," which occurred during the spring and summer of 1944. It has never clearly been dubbed a "round," though it deserves to be, as all the constituent elements are present: the demand for the three key ministries, negotiations, and the application of force (even if, in this case, violence was not done at the direct command of the KKE). I am referring to the sequence of events which began with the establishment, during the month of March 1944 in the mountains of "Free Greece," of the Political Committee of National Liberation, PEEA; which continued a few weeks later with the mutiny of the Greek Armed Forces in the Middle East, toppling the Government-in-Exile; and which ended in the confrontation between the new Premier of the Government, Papandreou, and the Communist Party of Greece, over the "National Charter" formulated at the Lebanon Conference.

ELAS' failure to crush EDES during the winter of 1943/44 marked the end of the First Round. During the spring of 1944 the KKE faced practically the same dilemma as that of the summer of 1943. It enjoyed everything but political legitimacy. It ruled the territories occupied by ELAS. It operated a civil administration, and commanded an army. But its control was not legitimate: *not recognised as legal by the Great Allies*. Legality remained the jealously guarded privilege of the Greek Government-in-Exile in Cairo, the Cabinet of which was dominated by the bourgeois republican coterie of Sophocles Venizelos.

I can think of very few Greek politicians who were less deserving of responsible positions in government than was Sophocles Venizelos. A weak man, devoid of imagination and initiative and unconcerned with the formulation of a programme of social reform to better the lot of the impoverished Greeks, Venizelos was an example of much that was wrong in the bourgeois political world.

How, then, to strip this sorry man of the legitimacy he so illegitimately possessed? This was the question confronting the KKE. The method chosen was politically to isolate Venizelos, in order to demonstrate just how unrepresentative the old bourgeois political leaders in reality were. If prominent Greeks from a broad spectrum of political persuasion could be enticed into collaboration with EAM, then EAM would appear to be the representative of the Greek masses — and Venizelos, isolated and terrified, would not put up much of a fight.

To isolate the Greek Government-in-Exile and so weaken its claim to legitimacy: this, then, was the objective of the KKE when, during

March 1944, it established PEEA. It was a direct challenge to the Government-in-Exile, for it was a Government in everything but name. Its officials were called Secretaries, rather than Ministers, but their power was real, in fact in many ways more real than the power of the Ministers in Cairo. Its programme of action, too, certainly was the programme of a government — of a social-democratic Government: free elections to a constituent assembly, a free plebiscite on the monarchy, territorial claims against Bulgaria and Albania, social justice *but* respect for private property, respect for religion. In April Greece's most prominent Socialist joined the Committee, Alexandros Svolos, a man with little political experience and no organsation at his command, but a man with great prestige, and even greater dreams. A former Liberal, too, joined the Committee: PEEA could now claim the allegiance of peasant, proletarian and shopkeeper! It constituted the perfect tool with which the Communist Party of Greece could achieve power.

For let there be no doubt that it was the KKE which wielded power within PEEA. The Political Committee was merely another manifestation of the "Popular Front" tactics so successfully employed by the Party in, for instance, the formation of EAM itself. What was sought was the participation of the greatest possible number of socialist and bourgeois figures in an organisation which, superficially, should appear to be a coalition of equal partners, but which in reality, would be a political machine under the control of the Party. Surely now, 34 years later, we must recognise that the Political Committee was in the hands of the Party? In fact it would be an insult to Greek Communism to suggest otherwise. One has only to sweep away the grand titles so generously bestowed upon the Socialist Svolos — he was made President of PEEA, Secretary for Foreign Affairs, Secretary for Popular Enlightenment! Indeed, it is amazing to think how this dreamy man carried so many portfolios on his shoulders — one has only to sweep all this tomfoolery aside and grasp the *fact* that George Siantos, Secretary of the Communist Party, was PEEA's Secretary *for the Interior,* to realise whose vote really counted.

How very great a threat was posed to the predominance of the bourgeois political world by the Political Committee, was immediately perceived by Tsouderos, the Premier of the Government-in-Exile, banker, republican, and rival of Sophocles Venizelos. The political isolation of the Government was what Tsouderos feared, and so he appealed to Themistocles Sofoulis, chief of the Liberals and leader of the bourgeois republican parties, to acquiesce in the inclusion in the Government of some resistance elements. After all, two could play the game of "popular front," and the Government, just as well as the Communists, could flatter a few "patriotic" guerrillas with innocuous ministries, and so bolster its claim to be representative. But Sofoulis would have nothing to do with this. In effect, he replied that the Government must remain the sole preserve of the old political world; as for EAM-ELAS and the threat it posed, he quite explicitly demanded that the Allies compel the resistance movement to obey the Government by withholding from them if necessary all supplies.

Sofoulis' decision sealed the doom of the Government-in-Exile, for the old political world, the bourgeois parties, *were* unrepresentative of the Greeks, and could not hope to survive except in collaboration with the new forces arising within the resistance movements. Yet to collaborate with the resistance movement meant to participate in such a radical reorganisation of the Greek economy, such a radical redistribution of Greek wealth, as to destroy the foundations of the bourgeois parties themselves. I am not referring only to the natural refusal of Sofoulis to collaborate with the KKE: I am referring to the incapability of Sofoulis to collaborate even with moderate Socialists, such as Svolos. Sofoulis represented old, bourgeois Greece, but the people of Greece were marching to goals beyond. Sofoulis gave Tsouderos the only reply he could: hold on tight, and get the Allies to disarm "this mob".

Sofoulis' decision had nothing to do with the King of Greece. It has often been argued that if only the King had abdicated, then all the old parties would have joined the Government, the people of Greece would have rallied to their side, the Communists would have been isolated and a moderate democracy would have been guaranteed. But this argument is fallacious. Let us imagine that the King had abdicated, and that subsequently every republican bourgeois politician in occupied Athens had descended on Cairo and joined the Government. Would they, then, have been more willing to collaborate with Socialists? I must answer no. Would the Government have been more representative? Certainly not. It was not that Tsouderos singly was unrepresentative, or that Venizelos singly was unrepresentative – the whole pre-war bourgeois political world was unrepresentative, and no matter how much larger its contingent in Cairo might have been had the King abdicated, the Government-in-Exile was doomed.

The end came swiftly, only some three weeks after the establishment of PEEA, and the executioners were masters of their profession. It hardly matters that the mutiny was not launched at the express command of the KKE. It was launched at the proper moment, by organisations within the Greek Armed Forces long associated with EAM-ELAS. The Communist Party during the war never denounced the munity, and had the Lebanon Conference gone a bit differently certainly would not have hesitated to exploit its result.

For its result was the collapse of the Government-in-Exile. Tsouderos, seeking desperately to defuse the mutiny in its early stages, issued an invitation to all parties and resistance movements to come to the Middle East to negotiate the formation of a broader Government. Yet this gesture came too late. Venizelos, exhibiting remarkably poor judgement, shattered the Government by exploiting the mutiny to overthrow

Tsouderos and grasp the premiership himself. But the Commander-in Chief of the Greek Army quit rather than impose discipline, and the Commander-in-Chief of the Navy and Venizelos then lost their nerve.

No matter what one's political persuasion, one must respect the efficiency with which the communist organisers of the mutiny razed the Government. First Tsouderos' dismissal was demanded and support given to Venizelos; no sooner had Venizelos taken over than Roussos, a Leftist Liberal, was called for; yet Roussos' candidature was barely a day old when it, too, was rejected as unsatisfactory. On 12 April 1944, when the King arrived in Cairo, the Government-in-Exile had ceased to exist. PEEA, and through it the Communist Party, remained as the sole governor of Greece.

If the story had come to an end here, this would have been "The Second Round," and a round ending in victory for the Communist Party. No less than a revolution had taken place, for power had passed from the old bourgeois world to the KKE. By a combination of extraordinary political pressure and well-exercised violence, the Communists had deftly isolated, demoralised and finally demolished the Government. Meanwhile they joined hands with Greece's most prominent Socialist, broadening their appeal and enhancing their claim to be the true representatives of the Greek people. Yet they had taken the precaution of monopolising all real power in their own hands, lest Svolos, by some social-democratic absurdity, hand Greece back to the Reaction.

But the story was not to end here and, indeed was to continue in a manner inimical to the interests of Greek Communism. The old political parties had never been a real danger; all of Greece was passing them by. Now a real opponent appeared, selected by the King as the new Premier of the Government-in-Exile, an opponent who threatened to isolate the KKE just as completely as the latter had isolated the bourgeois parties. This man was George Papandreou, and the danger he posed to the KKE is evident in the name of the Party he led: the Democratic-Socialist Party.

Papandreou, during 1944, represented Social-Democracy. He was just that one critical step to the Left beyond the old bourgeois world, to be a new phenomenon. He was young, full of zest and leadership, and in his first broadcast to occupied Greece he promised the people what Tsouderos and Venizelos never had had the courage — or the desire — to promise, social justice, a redistribution of income, a post-war Greek economy on a more egalitarian basis. And parliamentary democracy as well: free elections, a free plebiscite, liberty, security. For the first time a Premier of the Government-in-Exile promised the Greeks a new deal — a new deal which, hitherto, had been championed only by EAM-ELAS.

Just that critical step to the Left of the old bourgeoisie he was — yet also that much to the Right of Svolos that he would not countenance participation in PEEA. Nor was he a political neophyte, as was the Socialist. Papandreou knew the difference between being a President and being a figurehead. It was the combination of his commitment to reform and his political expertise which rendered him a mortal danger to the Communists, for he could match point for point when it came to their promises of social reform and democracy, yet he was out of their control.

Was he sincere? Or was he out for himself, a liar, or even a "Royalist lackey?" I believe he did wish sincerely to lead Greece to a more just society. It is true that he was not a theoretician, that he worked within no precisely defined ideological framework, and if one judges politicians from the standpoint of ideological purity, Svolos deserves more respect. But Svolos was a dreamer, capable of building Socialism only in his head, whereas Papandreou was a man of action, of practical politics. Whatever the nature of the regime Papandreou might have created, it would have been a far more liberal and egalitarian regime than that of the Greek bourgeoisie. On the other hand, it would have been further to the Right than the regime of Svolos, to be sure — but *so would have any regime*, because the regime of the non-entity Svolos would in reality have been the rule of the Communist Party.

Indeed, if anyone were insincere in his proclamations it was George Siantos. Are we really to believe that Greek Communists struggled and sacrificed and fought and died throughout World War II, for the sake of a multi-party parliamentary system of government? This is really to insult Greek Communism. Was not the KKE the vanguard of the revolutionary proletariat? With the Greek bourgeois parties crushed and the masses in arms under the banner of EAM, are we really to believe that the KKE looked forward to nothing more than a return to the "pigsty" of parliamentary politics? Siantos and Ioanidis — these men did not conceive of themselves as disciples of the Second International!

But they could not breathe a word about a dictatorship of the proletariat, about collectivism, soviet democracy, in a land of peasants. On the contrary, they had to talk about parliaments, about religion, about the sacred rights of property, if they were to win any support. Siantos had to speak like a "peaceful transition" Socialist, and this he did. *The whole programme of PEEA was social-democratic.* And so long as the bourgeoisie were PEEA's sole opponents, this tactical insincerity worked wonders. It gathered huge masses under the banner of EAM-ELAS; it attracted prominent Socialists, too. It worked very well, until Papandreou came along, and, in the name of the Government-in-Exile, began to sing the same refrain.

Singing PEEA's song is exactly what Papandreou did when politicians of all persuasions but Royalist, responding to Tsouderos' invitation, gathered in the Lebanon during mid-May 1944, to negotiate the formation of a new government. Had not PEEA demanded that the future of the Monarchy be decided by the People? Papandreou promised a free plebiscite. PEEA wanted the Greeks to pronounce upon the nature of their post-war social regime, and Papandreou undertook to conduct free elections to a constituent assembly. PEEA had championed Greek territorial claims — these Papandreou pledged to pursue to the full. And PEEA had called upon all guerrilla armies to unite under a single command. This Papandreou also did, but with the proviso that the command be the Government's, and not PEEA's. PEEA's programme was Papandreou's programme, but with one crucial difference: the Communist Party had intended that *it* should be the final judge of how "free" an election was, how truly "united" an army was. It had never been intended that a social-democrat, and an independent social-democrat, should pull the strings.

Svolos bolted to Papandreou's side at the Lebanon Conference, and considered the latter's programme to be the product of real statesmanship. He insisted that he had not gone to the mountains to strengthen the Communists, but rather to seek to prevent them from monopolising the Greek Left-wing movement. Now the chance had arrived to prevent that monopoly: Papandreou and Svolos, upstanding progressive democrats, and not the Bolsheviks, would implement PEEA's programme. The Democratic-Socialist and the Socialist, united in an effort to restore parliamentary democracy to Greece — the Communists' "Popular Front" had been shattered.

Petros Rousos, the representative of the Communist Party at the Lebanon Conference, to this day lives under the cloud of what he did at Lebanon. In fact he is lucky to be alive at all, if Ioanidis is to be believed. According to the latter, not a few voices in the mountains cried to have Rousos shot for putting his name to the "National Charter."

Yet Rousos committed no mistake at the Lebanon Conference, for when he acquiesced in Papandreou's adoption of PEEA's programme, there was nothing else he could have done. Rousos did not succumb to Papandreou's eloquence. He was not hypnotized, misled, or deluded. If his act had been due to confusion, then he could have been blamed for what he did.

No, what Rousos confronted, alone in the hills of Lebanon, was the entire war-time strategy of the Communist Party gone wrong. During the war the KKE had built its mass appeal on a social-democratic platform. Now that that platform had been adopted by the legal Government, what was Rousos to do — suddenly reveal the KKE's allegiance to Marxist-Leninist doctrine? Not only was it too late, it would have been entirely contrary to "popular front" tactics had he denounced Papandreou and, particularly, Svolos. Rousos made the correct decision at the Lebanon, and that was to sign the Charter and agree to join Papandreou's Government.

The key man at the Conference was Svolos. Who ever enjoyed the favour of the Socialist had the wider coalition, the greater claim to be the representative of the Greeks and hence the greater claim to legitimacy, and the easier task of appearing democratic. Papandreou won the day because he won Svolos. Rousos, isolated, had to bid soviet democracy goodbye.

But all this was, after all, just a conference, and a long way from reality. It was a tactical victory for Papandreou but a long way from triumph. For back in the mountains of Greece, Siantos took one look at the "National Charter," and threw it out.

It was the strength of Svolos at the Lebanon conference which made Rousos accept the Charter. It was the weakness of Svolos in the real world of politics which made Siantos reject it. For Siantos was the first to know that Svolos, other than prestige, possessed nothing: no mass organisation, no army, not even a party. He was a well-respected, sincere, trustworthy nobody. And as for Papandreou, he was a respected, perhaps insincere, definitely untrustworthy nobody. Svolos and Papandreou said they would conduct free elections. Yet how could they guarantee that? In over 100 years Greece had barely ever experienced a free election. What made these two newcomers to the upper echelons of Greek politics, without party, without physical power, so special that they could ensure that elections would be free? The Lebanon Charter was a moderate programme, yet *no organised, and powerful moderate centre existed in Greece.* Just how, then, was this Charter to be implemented?

Furthermore, who wanted so-called "free" elections anyway? Who wanted a so-called "moderate" policy? In the view of the Communist Party, Greece was passing into a new era ripe for a regime of workers and peasants. Multi-party elections and parliamentary democracy could only give reactionaries an opportunity to entice a predominantly peasant population off their revolutionary course. Indeed, is not that the precise Communist definition of a so-called "moderate" policy: misguided action, half-measures lacking in revolutionary decisiveness, absurd, legalistic, parliamentary mumbo-jumbo which blunts and betrays the masses' drive for power, and leaves them a confused, helpless prey to Reaction?

The Communist Party had espoused a social-democratic platform purely as propaganda, to delude a mass of peasants — presumably for their own good. It was a confidence trick. Now that an orator, and a dreamer, had adopted that platform as their own, was Siantos really expected to start to take it seriously?

By telegram, on 2 July, Siantos instructed the now bewildered "President" Svolos to inform Papandreou of EAM's "final conditions" for cooperation with the Government. PEEA, Siantos insisted, must be granted the Ministry of the Interior, the Ministry of Justice, and the Under-Secretariat of Defence. "They want us to surrender Greece." Papandreou declared, and indeed they did. Siantos demanded what the KKE had always demanded and, in fact, what they were to demand again, during December 1944: the three key ministries of Government.

And there matters stood when, as Elisabeth Barker describes, big power politics came into play and the Russian Military Mission arrived in Greece. After that, the KKE stance changed radically: they immediately agreed to enter the Government, without the key ministries. But the objective of the Communist Party had not changed. The quest for power continued, once again by negotiation at Caserta and in Athens, and by force all over Greece during December 1944.

The Mistakes of the Allies and the Mistakes of the Resistance

Andreas Kedros

(paper delivered in Greek)

Compared with the other resistance movements in the occupied countries during World War II, Greek resistance is characterised by some major features:

a. Widespread appeal: On 5 July 1943 the Athens *Abwehr* states in its secret report Ia Br. B. No.17512/44* that "80% of the Greeks are united in their hostility towards the occupying forces and ready to resist openly." No other European resistance movement has received from the enemy such a certificate of patriotism.

b. Effectiveness: The mass demonstrations of February and March 1943 in Athens and in the other major Greek cities against the civilian mobilisation decreed by Hitler were paid for in dozens of deaths and hundreds of injured. As a result Greece was the only country in occupied Europe where the Nazis did not succeed in imposing forced labour.

On several occasions, the various Greek resistance movements — particularly when they acted in concert, as after the creation of the united partisan H.Q. — made a decisive contribution to the Allied cause. During the summer of 1943, for instance, the strenuous activities of the Greek partisans led the High Command *Oberkommando* of the *Wehrmacht* to make a mistake. Thinking that the Allies were going to land somewhere on the Greek coast, they sent reinforcements of two divisions to mainland Greece and an elite battalion to Crete. The Germans were in desperate need of these forces when the Allies landed in Sicily. General Wilson recognised this explicitly as a congratulatory telegram which he sent to the HQ of the Greek partisans on 18 July 1943. On the eve of the liberation of Greece, the 30,000 EAM-ELAS partisans had under their control, with the exception of Athens and Thessaloniki, the majority of cities and almost the whole of Greek territory. The 5,000 EDES partisans

---

* This is the standard number of German *Abwehr* documents. For the document in quotation see A. Kedros 'Histoire de la Résistance Grecque.' Laffont *Paris*, 1966, p.291.

occupied part of Epirus, but they had started to collaborate with the Germans since the beginning of 1944 (See XII Nazi Division HQ document A.K. of 5 March 1944 1). Regrettably, ELAS had disbanded the 5/42nd regiment of Colonel Psarros with 2,000 partisans in April 1944.

c. Innovative social activities: EAM-ELAS experimented in the areas controlled by them with a kind of advanced self-governed democracy suggestive of what Tito was to introduce in Yugoslavia after the war. Thanks to its organisation and functioning, this experiment was successful among the villagers concerned.

How is it then, that a resistance movement so widely-based, effective (therefore useful to the Allies) and innovative, ended in such a historical disaster? How is it that the Greek people, after great sacrifices in the war (it is estimated that in the war in Albania, the resistance, and the horrible famine of the 1941-42 winter, the Greeks lost 800,000-1,000,000 men, women and children out of a pre-war population of 7,000,000) were brought to a civil war: that they were frustrated for decades in their attempts at a real democracy and that, even today, the title of 'partisan' is not recognised and honoured in Greece, but, on the contrary is dishonourable and a social stigma?

The responsibilities for this tragedy are divided. I will touch briefly upon a few of these. During World War II, Churchill was a providence-sent leader for the British people: an incomparable statesman and strategically his genius made it possible for the British to face the enemy successfully at a crucial time in their history. But in another sense, Churchill has been for the Greeks the architect of the greatest historical frustration a people has ever known. Because in Greece, during the Occupation and after the liberation, Churchill engaged in highly influential power politics which deliberately rebuffed the strongest aspirations of the vast majority of the Greeks. In the last 50 years there have been numerous examples of Western statesmen who, strongly attached to democracy in their own countries, indulged in power politics abroad, serving interests which we have no choice but to call imperialist. Most often these policies tend to install, or to maintain, in small or developing countries military regimes, dictatorial or pseudo-democratic, which serve the interest of the great power concerned. The wars in Algeria and Indochina, the interventions in Santo-Domingo, in Indonesia or in Chile are obvious examples.

Churchill was obsessed by two ideas; to keep the Russians out of the Mediterranean basin and to preserve the 'imperial road' to India and to oil. Churchill was, in some respects, a 19th century man. Despite Churchill's policy of "containing" the Russians which was subsequently transmuted into the Cold War and continues to haunt the West, Churchill nevertheless committed several mistakes.

He did not see the inevitable change in, not to say the breakdown of the British Empire and he did not foresee that the Arab-Israeli conflict would block the Suez Canal. He therefore over-estimated the strategic importance of Greece for the defence of British interests. On the other hand he under-estimated the antipathy which Greeks feel towards a Russian-style Communism. The Greeks invented democracy and are attached to it by temperament. Individualists, even anarchists, they revolt against hierarchy and constraint. Moreover Greece is essentially agricultural, as the country of 'garden produce' in the broad sense of the word, where the olive-tree, the vine, tobacco and rice are cultivated. These are crops incompatible with bureaucratic organisation in *Kolkhoz* or *Sovkhoz*.

However, after the long darkness of the Ottoman occupation and with the exception of some rare periods (like that of Venizelos) the Greeks have never seen their democratic aspirations realised. The royalist *coups de force*, the military *coups d'état*, the fascist regime of Metaxas, the Occupation, succeeded each other only to serve foreign interests. During the Occupation the Greeks, taking into account the declared objectives of the Allies, hoped to be able to take their own destiny in their hands, to live in a state of liberty, equality and progress. They were mistaken because Churchill himself was mistaken.

In his eyes the aim of EAM-ELAS, the major resistance movement, was to install in Greece a communist regime. This analysis was profoundly wrong. The communists were experienced militants and certainly devoted to their cause. They assisted the resistance with their experience of underground warfare; they were exceptionally brave, even heroic, disciplined, tireless and intransigent. They controlled ELAS but they were only a handful. Their struggle for national liberation and advanced democracy was sufficiently realistic and flexible to attract 80% of the Greek people as the *Abwehr* document states. In 1944 EAM-ELAS counted in its ranks – 6 bishops, a great number of priests, 30 university professors, 16 generals, 34 colonels and 500 officers of lower rank, all of them non-communists.

Was Churchill unaware of these facts or did he not wish to take them into account? The fact is that the intervention of the British troops during the invasion of Greece by the Nazi divisions had no strategic or even tactical value whatsoever. 'We must liberate Greeks – wrote Churchill to Eden on 6 March 1941 – from feeling bound to reject German ultimatums. If on their own they resolve to fight, we must to some extent share their ordeal" (Churchill: 'The Second World War' volume 3 p.92). This symbolic intervention can only be explained by ulterior political motives. Churchill was taking a risk – he was launching a "take-over bid" against post-war Greece. In his eyes, undoubtedly, this gesture apparently gratuitous (but very expensive in human lives) justified in advance the fact that Great Britain was to chain post-war Greece securely to British imperial policies. For Churchill the link in this chain was King George II. Ignoring the fact that the king had been the grave-digger of Greek democracy and the pillar of the Metaxas fascist regime, Churchill defended him against all winds as the depository of the sovereignty and legitimacy of the Greek state. General Wilson was much more objective in his valuation: 'Our position in Greece in 1941 — he wrote — was really a paradox that in our struggle against totalitarianism, we should be supporting one Fascist government against another.' (Wilson of Libya: 'Eight Years Overseas', London 1948. p.75).

As the Greek policy of Churchill crystallised so the will of the resistance and of the numerous political parties crystallised in the opposite direction — to oust this same king. In the eyes of many Greeks democracy and republicanism are more or less identical. (We shall see later on that this confusion of facts and vocabulary led to fatal simplifications). Be that as it may, in August 1943, in Cairo, all the representatives of the main resistance movements and also the members of the Greek Government in exile who represented the traditional parties, unanimously required that the King should make a binding declaration to return to the country only after the organisation of a referendum. Churchill and under his influence, Roosevelt, ridiculed the unanimous political will of the Greek people as expressed through their representatives. They assured the King of their unconditional support and urged him not to bind himself with a declaration.

It must be said that, in adopting this historically scandalous attitude, Churchill was self-consistent. Indeed, since April 1943, the SOE in Cairo notified Brigadier Myers, chief of the BMM to the partisans, that 'after the liberation of Greece, civil war is almost inevitable.' (E.C.W. Myers: 'Greek Entanglement,' London 1955, p.189).

This means that Churchill was prepared to take all risks and to consider the worst solutions in order to secure his objectives in Greece through, amongst other means, the return of the King.

Churchill's determination of August 1943 resulted in the revolt of the democratic soldiers of the Greek army in the Middle East. Twenty thousand fighters who had proved themselves in the battle of El Alamein were deported to Libya and elsewhere depriving the allied war effort of their potential. It probably also influenced the most opportunist elements of the resistance (and particularly of EDES) and of the Greek population, who knowing now which way the wind was blowing, opposed EAM-ELAS thereafter to the extent of openly collaborating with the Greek Quislings and the Occupation forces.

If, at the very moment when the resistance was at its peak, unanimous in its political will, Churchill cold-bloodedly envisaged a civil war in Greece after the liberation as an inexorable fact, we can understand why the parachuting of British arms to EAM-ELAS was always done with parsimony. Nevertheless the collapse of Mussolini's Italy allowed the EAM-ELAS partisans to take into their possession an important quantity of arms coming from the Italian Occupation army.

This chain reaction was not foreseen by Churchill. It upset his plans and forced him to manoeuvre. The first thing he was compelled to do was to secure his "rear". As early as April 1944 Churchill proposed to Stalin an agreement according to which the Russians were to exercise "preponderant control" in Romania, whereas the British were to exercise the same "preponderant control" in Greece. Stalin stipulated that the agreement be concluded only with the consent of the Americans. Cordell Hull, Secretary of State for the USA, was absolutely opposed to this division into "spheres of influence" but Roosevelt ignored the objections of his Secretary and endorsed the Churchill-Stalin agreement "for the duration of the war." The arrangement was to be concluded in June 1944 and confirmed in September of the same year.

Having obtained a 'free hand' in Greece, Churchill manoeuvred in the direction of EAM-ELAS which, meanwhile, had established PEEA, a kind of provisional government consisting of personalities of the left. The Greek government in exile had been headed for a short time by a new man: George Papandreou. With Churchill's consent Papandreou proposed to PEEA to send delegates to a conference in the Lebanon to form a Government of National Unity. However, he took advantage of the meeting to denounce EAM before world public opinion as responsible for the mutiny of the Greek forces in the Middle East as well as for the disbanding of the 5/42nd Regiment and the assassination of Colonel Psarros. Put on the defensive, the delegates of PEEA signed the 'Lebanon Agreement' which gave EAM-ELAS 5 ministerial posts out of 20 of the less important ones in the Government of National Unity. At their return to the partisans the delegates were denounced by the CC of EAM. Indeed EAM had just received information about a British plan which envisaged the annihilation of ELAS (C.M. Woodhouse: 'Apple of Discord.' London 1948, p.194). EAM published 18 months later all the telegrams exchanged between Cairo and the BMM on this subject. Meanwhile the arrival of a Soviet Military Mission to the resistance forces caused a complete turn about of the KKE and of the EAM leaders. Everything happened as if the Soviets had taken up the cause of Papandreou and Churchill, but leaving EAM-ELAS ignorant of the "arrangement" concluded in Moscow. Everything also happened as if this infamous deed was thereafter to precipitate the leadership of EAM from one mistake to another. Not only did they accept participation in the Government of National Unity under the terms imposed by Papandreou, but at Caserta they signed a document which subjected all the resistance forces to the command of the British General Scobie. These arrangements may appear consistent with the Churchill-Stalin agreement, but they nonetheless undermined all that the Greek people had fought for during the Occupation.

From the very first, even before Yalta, Churchill (as we are going to see), Stalin and even Roosevelt exercised a Great Power policy of spheres of influence which was in complete contradiction to the principle of popular self-determination solemnly proclaimed in the Atlantic Charter. They made in vain the sacrifice of thousands of partisans shot, tortured, imprisoned, or deported by the Occupation forces and of hundreds of thousands of other Greeks who died from starvation in a poor country, crushed under the heel of the innumerable Nazi, Italian and Bulgarian armies, cut off from any supplies from abroad because of the allied blockade. This policy resulted in turning the Greek partisans against the British liberation forces and subsequently threw the entire Greek population into civil war. It also had the consequence of maintaining a fascist state mechanism, inherited from Metaxas and the collaborators, which under the cover of pseudo-democracy would for decades take revenge upon those men who had performed their patriotic duty and who, everywhere else in Europe, were honoured, compensated and elevated to the highest offices.

Should we conclude that the resistance movement bears no responsibility for this sequence of events? To affirm this would be to lack objectivity. On several occasions the resistance, and in particular EAM-ELAS, held the key to much better solutions than those selected, which could have thwarted or at least lessened the effects of the ill-omened policies of the Great Powers.

The first mistake, particularly of EAM and parallel to that of Churchill, was to elaborate the entire policy advocated for the post-war period around the person of the King. The statutes of EAM had comprised, from the very beginning, a kind of declaration against not only the Occupation forces but also against monarchy as an institution. It is understandable that in EAM's eyes the anti-fascist struggle had also to be against a fascist king and a fascist government. But to link the democratization of the country (the principal objective of EAM-ELAS) in such a narrow way to a referendum which would abolish monarchy was to rule out many possibilities for future manoeuvre. The recent history of Greece and even Greek vocabulary identify 'republic' with 'democracy'. But in the modern world this identification appears to be schematic. Democracy (in England, Denmark, Sweden and now in Spain) is not incompatible with monarchy, provided that the latter is reduced by appropriate measures to a purely symbolic function. Such a democracy could have been envisaged in Greece, at least as a transitional stage, and could have reduced antagonisms in the country and, more importantly among the partisans, which were often only formal if not altogether artificial. In the reverse sense this is how the colonels proceeded in the 70's when they decided to get rid of the King. The EAM-ELAS leaders faced with the complexity of the historical tasks which they had shouldered did not strike the right balance between tactics and strategies. Making monarchy the absolute alternative to any democratic regime they sacrificed tactics to strategy and gave ammunition to their opponents. (In this domain Tito knew better how to get out of a scrape).

The second mistake of EAM-ELAS, a consequence of the first, was to allow the development inside the resistance movement of an embryonic civil war. Certainly EDES received favourable treatment from the BMM. Certainly this movement became in the end a kind of praetorian guard for the BMM. Certainly General Zervas, head of EDES, secretly sent a telegram of allegiance to the King. Without doubt provocative actions encouraged clashes and, towards the end of the Occupation, by way of a mounting dialectic to which EAM-ELAS was no stranger, EDES ended up by throwing itself on to the side of the Germans. But the leaders of EAM-ELAS had not been able either to foresee or to contol this process. Otherwise, would they have left so much to Aris Velouchiotis? This brave man was an excellent organiser and also a manipulator of the masses but was suffering from the complex of all communist renegades. Under the Metaxas regime he had signed a declaration denouncing communism — and this led him to extremism, made him sectarian, and inclined always to go one better. Not just the assassination of Colonel Psarros but also many other violent actions which degraded the partisan movement have to be attributed to him. This is even more regrettable since the balance of power was favourable to EAM-ELAS, and would have allowed a flexible evolution, with a minimum of unnecessary sacrifices, towards its final objective: an advanced democracy. Instead, EAM-ELAS has always given the impression that, because of this mini-civil war which they appeared to favour (if they did not actually cause it) they opted for violent solutions.

Many of the mistakes of EAM-ELAS derived from the inability to adapt tactics and strategies to the real balance of power. Although they allowed themselves to be manoeuvred either by Papandreou or by the Soviet Military Mission or again at the time of the Caserta Agreement, by Churchill and his acolytes, EAM-ELAS had kept its armed force intact and had, in a political sense, enough cards to play to save the essentials.

Up to this day the surviving leaders of EAM-ELAS declare in the face of all evidence, that they did not have any choice. In fact there was a choice. EAM-ELAS, although handicapped by the unfavourable Churchill-Stalin agreements, could have chosen to rely on the resistance movement, its bastion, which controlled four-fifths of all Greek territory after the allies had landed in Greece. They could also have chosen to negotiate with the British and the Papandreou government and to defend their positions and their demands step by step in the course of negotiations which would have resulted in an acceptable compromise guaranteed by world public opinion. The truth is that the leaders of EAM-ELAS were not statesmen and did not know how to negotiate. So after spasmodic movements they ended with complete political capitulation because they were put in an untenable situation.

The inevitable happened. Sure of their "rights", properly informed but uneasy before the potent power, still intact, of the partisans the British offered cover and support to all those they could still count upon: the royalist remains of the Greek army of the Middle East, the Security Battalions organised by the Nazis, the collaborators in the police and the security forces, the "anti-communist" armed gangs.

When the British demanded that all these fascists join with the partisans — their opponents of yesterday — in a national army in conformity with the Caserta Agreement, the Government of National Unity collapsed. But once more EAM-ELAS made the wrong evaluation of the balance of power. The most intransigent of the leaders, under-estimating the capacity of the British forces to resist and Churchill's political will, confident of being able to count upon important reinforcements, in December 1944 launched against the British tanks badly-armed partisans cut off from their bases.

Defeated, these men fled Athens, commiting unnecessary atrocities. EAM-ELAS had lost a battle but not yet the war. But once more the leadership shamelessly capitulated. When they signed the Varkiza Agreement not only did they surrender to the British, with no compensation whatsover, the arms which the partisans had won heroically from the Occupation forces, but they also abandoned those who had followed them. Disarmed and with no defense the partisans became the victims of a "settlement of accounts". Accused of common crimes for every act of politically resistance made under the Occupation, thousands of men and women were imprisoned, deported, shot by the fascists — their opponents of yesterday. Under the shadow of British legitimacy gangs of militia turned without restraint upon the former partisans and without formal proceedings "liquidated" the militants and fighters of EAM-ELAS.

Naturally such a situation could not last for long: the "white terror" forced the old partisans to go underground. It led directly to civil war which in its turn was to block for decades all normal political development in Greece.

As we see, the mistakes and responsibilities are shared. The Allies sacrificed the Greek people to their Great Power politics. The leaders of EAM-ELAS, instead of avoiding the traps prepared for them, fell into them because of their political and historical myopia.

Translated by Anna Syngelakis
Edited by Jenny Wood

DISCUSSION

Bickham Sweet-Escott: I would not agree with you when you say that Churchill decided to intervene to assist the Greek Government against the Germans in order to make a "take-over bid" for post-war Greece.

Andreas Kedros (to B. Sweet-Escott): What would have happened if, despite Churchill's telegram to Eden, the Greeks had decided not to resist the Germans?

B. Sweet-Escott: I should think the answer to that is very simple — Greece would have been overrun by the Germans.

Andreas Kedros: That happened anyway. So what was the *rationale* of the whole thing from the military point of view?

Prof. Hammond: Could I answer that? I was in Greece in those early months of '41. The spirit of the Greeks was such that it would have been impossible not to resist the Germans. There was tremendous feeling in Greece and in Athens and I do not think that any government could have carried through a surrender to the Germans, or have attempted to do so. The victories over the Italians had given the Greek people great confidence. The Government which said *"Ochi"** to the Italians was the government headed by the King and Prime Minister Metaxas and it was the same government which decided to resist the Germans. From the British point of view, the Greeks came to the aid of Great Britain which was fighting alone against the Nazis and we owed great gratitude to Greece and still do. That was why we went in to help Greece both aganist the Italians and against the Germans. Possibly it was bad policy but it was an act of faith and of humanity and in effect it did delay the German attack on Russia at a vital point in the war. This left a legacy for both countries in that Britain had ties with the Government which became the Government-in-Exile and had a debt to pay to that Government which had come to our aid.

Andreas Kedros: Prof. Hammond, could you repeat the last sentence about the Greek Government?

Prof. Hammond: When the Greek Government withdrew from Crete it was still for Britain the official government of Greece.

Andreas Kedros: I think that the events which followed from then until Churchill's intervention against the whole of the Greek people in the persons of its representatives shows that this intervention had something more than a humanitarian element. When a statesman dares to say "No" to a whole people this cannot be considered an act of humanity. It was Churchill's intervention in Greece in 1940-41 — an intervention which required a certain courage — which served him as a justification for his later extremist stand. He had probably foreseen what was going to happen as he was a political and a military genius.

George Catephores: The paper regretfully assumed the responsibility of Aris Velouchiotis for the death of Psarros. But the fact is that Aris did not order it and certainly did not execute him. This is from information which has emerged since. Aris' personality had its faults but also

---

* The Greek word for "no"

its greatness. And we should not tax him with feats he did not perform and certainly not with crimes he did not commit.

Andreas Kedros: It is difficult for a historian to distinguish what is Aris' responsiblity and what is that of the people who gave him orders. I hold that he was responsible. First, he could have kept the leadership better informed; secondly, he could have stopped certain things from happening. But I should like to reply more generally about what I have called a mini civil war in the mountains. There the responsibilities were shared. The Communists have always said that marxism — their marxism — is a political praxis on a higher level than the praxis of other political parties and that this praxis is enriched by theory and can itself enrich theory. This means that their strategy and tactics should have been better. So, when things go wrong, I personally tend to blame the marxists, the Communists, precisely because they are marxists.

Christos Alexiou: I would like to make three points. First, there is a contradiction in what Prof. Hammond said that no Greek Government could resist the Greek people's will to fight. If this was so, then it was not the Metaxas Government which said "No" but the Greek people. Yet Churchill was grateful only to the King and to that government but completely forgot the Greek people and went against their will. Secondly, I would like to say that ELAS controlled not only the mountains but the cities as well. Athens was almost completely controlled by the 1st Army Corps which was the unit which mainly fought the British in December 1944. As a member of ELAS, I myself went to many towns in Thessaly and I know that the Germans did not control the towns. Thirdly, there is a contradiction in what Mr. Kedros said about the EAM programme holding the key to better solutions to the political problem, even perhaps democracy under the King. But if the aims of EAM had been clearer, could EAM have won like Tito did? I think yes. But you, in your paper, say no.

Andreas Kedros: I said — but let's emphasise it again — that the Germans did not control any town except Athens and Salonica. As for Tito, he was in a much more favourable position but still he had to manoeuvre very adroitly.

Richard Clogg: You said that, at the end, the British gathered together all the fascists with the remnants of the Greek army in the Middle East and wanted to combine these with the partisans into a National Army. My question is: would you call Tsigantes* a fascist?

Andreas Kedros: When we talk about the remnants of the Greek army, we should remember that these people were dedicated to the King and consequently to the regime of the dictator Metaxas. There is no doubt that among these royalists there were people like Tsigantes, the ex-

---

* The late General Christos Tsigantes, a former republican officer, compulsorily retired after 1935, who went to the Middle East during the Occupation and gravitated towards royalism.

ceptions, who, though they were for the King, had not a fascist mentality. But the officer corps in the aggregate later showed itself fascist-minded. It attacked the Resistance as viciously as did the purely fascist gangs.

EAM-ELAS: Resistance or National Liberation Movement?

Thanasis Hajis
(paper delivered in Greek)

When the Germans entered Greece they expected to find a strong state imbued with the ideals of fascism and a people who had already suffered much because they had been dragged into the war by the British — a people who would feel relieved because the war was over. The Germans expected that their troops would be greeted at least with acquiescence, if not with friendship and solidarity. This explains the words used by the first German governor of Athens Scheiben when he addressed the representatives of the Greek state: "We have not come as enemies, we have come as friends. Our long-standing friendship with Greece will be revived within a few days. Continue to exercise your power and the *Wehrmacht* will support you wholeheartedly". Furthermore Hitler, under the illusion that he could use Greece and the Greek people for his future plans, praised the gallantry of the officers and men of the Greek army and very magnanimously decreed that no Greek should become a prisoner of war.

It was not long before the Germans and their Italian and Bulgarian Allies realised that they had entered into a hostile country whose people felt bitter and hurt, not because of their defeat which they would not concede, but because of the treason perpetrated by the leaders of the nation. The first acts of disobedience must have opened their eyes to the fact that they were sitting on a volcano that sooner or later would erupt. Their reaction was inevitable: they had conquered Greece by force of arms — it was by force of arms that they would impose their authority and law and order throughout the Occupation.

Their authority rested on their arms, but this did not mean that demagogy did not have its uses. A government composed of Greeks who would serve the Occupation authorities faithfully and act as a kind of intermediary between the Germans and the people would be better than a German *Gauleiter*.

In all occupied countries ambitious and vile "scum", to use Hitler's phrase, were easily found. Such people existed in Greece as well. The old bourgeois politicians were thought by the Germans to be on the wane, and as such not useful. The "New Order" needed "dynamic personalities". In General Tsolakoglou the Germans thought they had found the Marshal Pétain of Greece.

The first Quisling "government" headed by Tsolakoglou was sworn in by Damaskinos who was later to become Churchill's favourite and Regent, and was promptly recognised as a "government of national necessity" by the representatives of all traditional bourgeois parties. Many personalities from "intellectual circles" connected with the notorious Institutions (Rectors of Universities and Schools of Higher Education, Academicians, etc.) as well as the higher clergy hastened to ally themselves with the "Government".

The first task of the "new national leadership" was to disarm the people morally in the name of "keeping order", so that people could accept their slavery and obey. 'Victory will be achieved if the national soul of all Greeks stays vigilant so that the concept of the state is preserved. If the social order is not overturned − this will constitute victory' wrote Tsolakoglou in one of his first orders to the security forces. 'Furthermore', he went on, 'we would like to stress the danger to society posed by the criminal elements whose numbers have grown, and the security forces are hereby instructed to remain vigilant against anything which may imperil order and the rule of law'. From the moment obedience to the conqueror became "order" and the "rule of law", treason must run its course. This so-called "Greek Government" was ignored and treated with contempt by the Greek people. From a legal viewpoint Greece, despite the creation of that monstrosity which posed as the government, never joined the Axis and remained throughout the war an occupied country. The setting up of the Tsolakoglou government was the first failure of the Germans. They did not succeed in establishing a government or a state power that would possess a semblance of legitimacy or would at least be tolerable to the people. The Greek state did not exist any more − it had been dissolved before the fronts collapsed. There was of course the royal government abroad which formally upheld the lawful position of Greece in the war − i.e. the side of Britain. This pro-royalist government was hated and ignored by the Greek people because it opposed the people, served the foreigners and was held responsible for the Metaxas dictatorship, its desertion of Greece and its subsequent treason.

There was no Greek state, no Greek authority. But in Greece the initial gestures of disobedience were followed by the first acts of passive and active resistance against the conquerors, and this created the need for a national leadership that would organise, coordinate and guide the resistance activity of the people so that the struggle would achieve maximum efficiency with minimum sacrifices. The traditional ruling class represented by the traditional political parties could not provide such a leadership. The members of the Greek Communist Party who were scattered around the country sensed this need, but they were hopelessly isolated − the leadership of KKE had stopped functioning. Without a single exception all the members of the KKE Central

Committee and most of the party cadres were either in prison, in exile on various islands or in prison camps. They had been betrayed and handed over to the conquerors by the monarcho-fascists. This is yet another proof of the treason perpetrated by the ruling oligarchy and the government of the deserters.

Many people, not only our enemies but also some friends of the people, have alleged that during the war KKE did not react before Hitler's attack on the Soviet Union. This allegation is based on the fallacy that the Central Committee of KKE did not issue any formal statement to the effect that the party would fight for national liberation together with the Greek people.

This allegation, if it is not made in bad faith, is to say the least baseless. It is well known that a group of cadres who presented themselves as a continuation of the party leadership, under the guidance of the Central Committee member Nikos Plumbidis who was still in prison, circulated a manifesto on the 3 May 1941, in other words 10 days after the Germans entered Athens, which *inter alia,* said the following: 'in order to liberate our country from the foreign yoke we must fight. This struggle must necessarily be based first of all on our heroic people united in the Front for National Salvation and Peace but at the same time on the alliance with other enslaved Balkan people, and on the help of the great Soviet Union. . .' Addressed to the communists, the youth of the country and those who were likely to be sympathetic to their cause, the manifesto went on to say: 'The time has come for you to show to the slanderers. . . how the communists fight for their country. . . Place yourselves at the head of the popular struggle for national liberation. . .' The manifesto also addressed patriotic officers and NCOs: 'Those who sit back and expect England to free us, or wait for the conqueror's good will — those people serve the purposes of the traitors. . .' And the manifesto stated categorically on behalf of KKE: 'We have taken our position in the ranks of the Front of Salvation and Peace and we stretch out our hand to all those who are willing to fight in order to rid our country of the foreign yoke through the struggle of our people side by side with the other Balkan people'.

Many details concerning the stand taken by the Independent Communist Organisation of Athens have been published. By July 1941 the Athens Organisation had already organised a mass demonstration by war-disabled and demobbed soldiers with national and economic slogans, and had formed a national liberation group which included officers and soldiers. Communist organisations and isolated communists in Macedonia, Thessaly, Epirus and the Peloponnese started to be active after the collapse of the front. They collected and hid arms, helped stranded British soldiers to escape capture and reach the Middle East, and carried out acts of sabotage. Almost all these first armed guerrilla units or self-defence groups were headed by communists who acted either under party instructions or on their own initiative. In Crete the communists were leading a massive armed resistance movement which was a continuation of the popular participation in the struggle against the Germans.

Following the first acts of active resistance, the first national liberation organisation on a nation-wide scale entered the scene. It is a well known and indisputable fact that in the last third of May 1941 the national liberation organisation "Freedom" was created in Salonica on the initiative of the members of the Macedonia District Bureau of KKE and with the participation of socialists, agrarians and the Mercourios group of officers. Colonel D. Psarros was placed at the head of the military branch of "Freedom". An address to the people was circulated at the beginning of June and somewhat later the underground newspaper *Freedom* started publication. At Athens on 21 May the first national-liberation organisation was formed under the name "National Solidarity", on the initiative of communists who had escaped from prison. During the occupation National Solidarity became the Red Cross of Greece with about 3,000,000 members and subscribers.

In my book 'The victorious revolution that was lost'* I have included a lot of evidence which refutes the slanderous allegation that KKE remained inactive during the first stages of the Occupation and then decided to resist, not for national reasons but in order to benefit the Soviet Union. KKE, whose members had been scattered all over the country began its struggle on the first day of the Occupation without any vacillations and reservations. The policy of the national-liberation front, with its national and social content, had already been formulated and accepted by all the Greek communists before the Soviet Union entered the war and before the 6th Plenum of KKE was held.

One point should be underlined however: the Communists, even without a central leadership accepted by everybody, did everything possible wherever they happened to find themselves and with every means at their disposal. They demonstrated their determination to continue the national liberation struggle at the head of the Greek people until the final defeat of fascism. It is to the credit of KKE that after 20 years of action it had created a sufficiently large number of cadres and members who were not only loyal and experienced, but also ideologically and politically ready and mature enough to cope with such a complex and difficult situation. Among the 200 or so cadres of KKE who escaped from the prisons and the islands there were four members of the Central Committee who had been elected by the 8th Congress. These four took a number of initiatives but did not have the courage to act as the KKE leadership. Thus the problem of leadership remained unsolved, although there was some progress in that direction following the suggestions of the Central Committee members who

---

* 'I Nikifora Epanastasi pou hathike' (1941-1945). 3v. *Athens*, 1977-80.

were still in the Akronauplia prison. A few days before Germany invaded the Soviet Union a group of Macedonian communists was released. Among them were Tsipas, an alternate member of the Central Committee, and two senior cadres, the trade unionist K. Lazarides and the former member of Parliament Tzimas. They reached Athens bringing a draft resolution which had been drawn up by the comrades in Akronauplia and the suggestion that a Plenum should be held so that a Central Committee could be formed immediately. Thus the 6th Plenum, was held and its resolutions were published dated 1 July 1941. These events and dates are significant. No *bona fide* observer should fail to notice that the main point of the resolution, i.e. the struggle for freedom, independence and popular sovereignty and the policy of a national front had been formulated by the members of the Central Committee held in Akronauplia before the Soviet Union entered the war. The "free' members of the Central Committee simply added the passage which deals with the new situation that had arisen with the entry of the USSR into the war, and I must admit that their assessment of it was not absolutely correct.

The concept of Resistance is usually identified with guerrilla war, armed clashes, sabotage and secret intelligence services, possibly as a result of the activities of the partisans in Yugoslavia, Albania, Russia etc. In Greece resistance assumed a much wider scope and displayed its own particular features. Resistance in Greece became a movement that embraced the whole of Greece and all the Greek people. Its manifestations were manifold: individual initiatives, popular committees, massive strikes and demonstrations by unarmed civilians, sabotage of enemy installations, sniper action by individuals, guerrilla units, partisans and a popular army which engaged the enemy in battle. In short, the national liberation movement in Greece was a combination of massive unarmed struggle and military activity. This dual character persisted until the end. Neither of these two aspects — armed or unarmed struggle — was predominant; they both materialised simultaneously and depending on the circumstances one or the other prevailed in each particular district.

These two fundamental expressions of the popular movement in Greece were not contradictory — and the development of one did not hinder the development of the other. On the contrary one can say that they are complimentary. In many cases they combined into a unitary form of popular insurrection, using all available means. There were many such examples in Greece. The ELAS reservists, the members of the National Militia, the members of EAM, EPON and other national liberation organisations stood shoulder to shoulder with the regular ELAS — and all the Greeks gave them active support. They all fought united under the command of the regular ELAS which together with the reserve ELAS were the main fighting force.

The Greek plutocrats and their foreign protectors did not want and could not fight such a war. They were afraid of the armed people and popular insurrection more than they were afraid of the Nazis. Throughout the foreign Occupation there were numerous examples of panic among the Greek and foreign reactionaries. Panic and their animosity and hatred against EAM even led them to open collaboration with the Nazis and the traitors or the British and their praetorian guard — the target always being EAM-ELAS. Most professional officers could not wage such a war and refused to join it. In keeping with their training and their former experience, they only believed in a war which would involve regular armies representing states. The participation of the popular masses, and even, more than that, the involvement of irregular armed citizens was denounced as "mutiny", as a breach of military rules and was considered detrimental to the manoeuvres of the regular armies. Only a popular leadership could inspire, organise and mobilise the whole of the people for the defence or the liberation of the country. Such a leadership was created on 27 September 1941 when EAM was founded. KKE provided EAM with its brains and backbone.

The question that must be answered is how did EAM manage to raise its membership to more than 2,000,000 and why was it supported by 95% of the Greek people?

In its brief but dignified and impassioned manifesto, EAM stated its principles and programme and determination to fight. Its ambition was to unite the whole nation; its aims were a fusion of the common national and political aims of Greek patriots. It was not an ideological manifesto and did not reflect a particular world view; in other words it was not a manifesto of a communist or socialist party. The EAM manifesto could be accepted by the masses, the various social classes and those who subscribed to different political and social ideologies. It was a programme for a democratic change in Greece which would introduce rule by the people based on national independence. According to EAM the liberation of the country and the safeguarding of its independence would depend primarily on the struggle of the Greek people without outside help. EAM regarded the national liberation struggle as a continuation of the war in Albania and Macedonia, and as a contribution by the Greek people to the fight of the allies against fascism. Thus EAM aligned the content of the national liberation struggle with the general war that the allies were fighting against the Axis powers.

EAM would not have been able to mobilise the people to such a wide extent both inside and outside Greece, it would not have succeeded in acquiring such power and winning the confidence of the people, had it not made it clear that the struggle would not be in vain. In its programme it declared that immediately after liberation EAM would form a government which would safeguard national independence against any foreign imperialist power. EAM effectively barred the plutocratic oligarchy from power. Now as regards the kind of regime and the form of government which would take over after the war, EAM declared that the people would decide freely through an elected sovereign constituent assembly. At the same time it gave a solemn warning by pledging: 'The safeguarding of this sovereign right of the Greek people to decide on the nature of its government against any reactionary attempt to impose on the people solutions contrary to its will. EAM and its organisations will use every means at their disposal to frustrate such an attempt.'

The above statement reveals the nature of the EAM struggle; it was a struggle for national liberation — against fascism — against imperialism — against plutocracy — and for the rule of the people. The power that would emerge would be the power of the people. In other words the EAM struggle was a revolution.

It is obvious that EAM did not include among the aims of its revolution the abolition of private property, and this means that it did not plan to overthrow the bourgeois regime. It was not however a bourgeois democratic revolution similar to those that had taken place before the Second World War in underdeveloped countries. Those revolutions were chiefly directed against feudalism or the residues of the feudal system and their aim was to introduce bourgeois democratic reform. Under the circumstances of the Second World War and according to the declarations of the Allies and, more importantly according to the practice of the popular masses, the main target of EAM was not so much the feudal residues. Its main target was the enemy and its main aims were to destroy fascism, to safeguard national independence free of any imperialist dependence, and to take power away from the traitors and collaborators of the upper middle class. The war and the Axis Occupation brought about the financial ruin of the middle classes and of a great part of the middle and lower strata of the bourgeoisie. This meant that the vast majority of the people felt inclined to accept the solutions proposed by EAM. If the nature of the revolution is determined, in the last instance, by the relative strength of the opposing forces, then we could say that the regime envisaged by EAM had a great chance to develop into a socialist revolution, without too many upheavals and confrontations.

The popular movement of EAM fought for the national and social liberation of Greece on the basis of its triple aim: Freedom—Independence — Rule by the people, linked directly to its struggle for survival. According to EAM the realisation of its aim depended on the victorious outcome of the war, but not necessarily on the actual intervention of allied (Anglo-American) forces in Greece or the advance of the Soviet armies. EAM carried out its struggle based on the resources of the Greek people, and this policy was justified by subsequent events. As it turned out there was no need for an allied invasion. ELAS with the help of the people took advantage of the Red Army advance in the Balkans and liberated the whole of the country. ELAS managed to drive the Germans out of all Greece, except a few square kilometres in Epirus which remained under Zervas. In other words EAM was not one of those resistance organisations well known to the west — it led a national liberation struggle in the full meaning of the term, a real national and popular revolution.

We have made this distinction in order to pose an historical question: the general term "resistance" or "national resistance" has been widely used when talking about the Second World War. We believe that this general usage does not accurately reflect the earth-shaking events that took place during the war. There were fundamental differences between the various movements that sprang up in Western Europe and the Balkans. In Western Europe the struggle against the occupation force has been referred to as "Resistance" or "National Resistance". This term was first coined by a group of French patriots who worked in the Musée de l'Homme in Paris. They decided after a lot of thought to use the word "Resistance" instead of "Liberation", and their organisation as well as the paper they published clandestinely was finally named "Resistance". According to the members of that group this was done for essential reasons: since France would be liberated mainly by the Anglo-American forces, the role of the struggle of the French patriot could not but be ancillary to the task of the allied troops. A little while later the term "Resistance" was used by De Gaulle in a broadcast he made from London. In the Balkans and in Greece the term "Resistance" was virtually unknown during the Occupation and was never used by EAM. The term did not correspond to the nature of the EAM movement. EAM regarded its struggle as a continuation of the national liberation war; it based its efforts on the forces inside the country, which would have liberated Greece, perhaps without the help of allied landings. While fighting against the Occupation forces EAM linked the liberation of Greece to the more general and permanent problem that beset Greece — the restitution of absolute national independence and safeguarding of such independence against any imperialist threat. This particular feature leads us to the explicit conclusion that the concept of a national liberation movement in Greece coincided with EAM.

Does this, however, mean that there were no other organisations or forces in Greece which resisted or inflicted casualties on the enemy? Certainly not. There were, for example, the forces of Zervas and EKKA and a multitude of secret organisations. They all resisted the enemy but did not carry out a national liberation struggle, Zervas too carried out resistance despite the fact that published documents from the German archives indicate that he entered into agreements and an armistice with the Germans. These organisations distinguished between the war and politics, thinking that they would deal with the latter after the liberation. Their existence depended directly on provisions sent by the Middle East HQ under whose command they had placed themselves. They carried out its orders exclusively and served British interests whole-heartedly. Very characteristic and revealing in that respect is the well-known pledge made by Zervas to Winston Churchill that he was willing to support the return of the King, even against the will of the Greek people, if it was necessary for the interests of Britain. In other words he was willing to strike against the Greek people, not only in defending the interests of the bourgeois regime but also the interests of Britain which was to come in, after the Germans had been driven out, in order to impose its own occupation on Greece. This statement was so disgraceful that even Colonel Woodhouse, an enemy of EAM, who in any case bore some of the responsibility for the appalling behaviour of his protégé, has referred to it in extremely uncomplimentary terms.

The British troops arrived in Athens after an "invitation" extended to them by the Papandreou government which included KKE and EAM ministers. The British did not fire a single shot against the Germans who were pulling out. The leadership of EAM accepted them as a "philanthropic" mission that would provide food and provisions for the people who were hungry and exhausted. EAM forgot the old saying: *Timeo Danaos et dona ferentes.* EAM did not assume full power when it was there for the taking; EAM-ELAS dominated Athens and there was no power, either Greek or foreign, that could challenge their domination.

This confirms that the EAM leadership abandoned its goal of gaining power through revolution. This does not of course imply that EAM did not pose the question of power.

This contradiction can be historically explained. As we have already said EAM, in its manifesto, did pose the question of power and its own brand of power structure was put into effect in every city and village liberated by ELAS through the setting up of committees of popular authority. Halfway through 1943 the EAM movement dominated the whole of Greece and the impact of its activities had been felt by the Greek army in the Middle East, by those Greeks who had emigrated or were working abroad and in the Dodecannese which had been annexed by Italy. The prestige of EAM was felt throughout Greece. Its army was strong, well organised, battle-trained and capable of liberating large districts where the new popular power would take root: a new concept of power, which was revolutionary and creative, unlike anything else that Greece had known. The old regime and its state had crumbled and the people, exercising their power, were removing its foundations. However, at the time when the people became conscious of their strength, when they believed that "the time had come" for a clean sweep in Greece — then the leadership of the EAM movement lost touch with the people. The postscript to the first volume of my book 'The victorious revolution that was lost' contains the following passage: 'It seemed that (the leadership) was no longer guided by the will of the working and oppressed masses. It seemed to stagger, vacillate and lose its way. Thus began the first doubts and hesitations and the first concessions to the British and to the Greek bourgeoisie. The EAM leadership thought that the British, the Cairo government and the traditional bourgeois parties carried *more weight than they actually did,* in a revolutionary and fully armed Greece. This first retreat under pressure from the adversary would lead to a compromise and the revolutionary march of the popular movement virtually came to an end.'

Thus the enormous and unprecedented EAM movement found itself in a curious predicament: on the one hand EAM-ELAS with the help of the people continued its national liberation struggle, liberated more and more areas and kept marching towards final victory and power, and on the other the leadership of the movement retreated, and after a series of mistakes and concessions turned its back on the revolutionary achievements of the people, recognised the bourgeois regime, put its faith in bourgeois parliamentary and constitutional procedures, accepted ministries in a government which was the puppet of foreigners and authorised the British to manage the internal affairs of the country. The British aim remained the same throughout the war: to dismantle the popular organisations, dissolve ELAS, disarm the people and fill the government with their creatures who would be willing to serve blindly the interests of imperialist Britain. These two contradictory political lines persisted until the end, and the contradiction facilitated the British military intervention in December 1944. When ELAS was forced to evacuate Athens its forces were still intact and it was still possible to continue the war outside the capital in order to secure, if not victory, then at least better terms for the people. Its leadership, however, was seized by panic and for that reason signed the disgraceful Varkiza Agreement. The victorious revolution was lost mainly because of the mistakes of our leadership. The British were jubilant and the reactionaries, spearheaded by the collaborators and the traitors of the Security Battalions, took their revenge on the people.

DISCUSSION

Question from the auditorium seeking clarification on a point of self-criticism: Mr Hajis has said that EAM-ELAS developed a sort of inferiority complex because they lost in 1944, that the EAM movement has been severely criticised and possibly damaged by this criticism. I would like to disagree because I believe that, to achieve a global perception of what happened, we should criticise not only the other side but ourselves as well.

*Thanasis Hajis:** There has been a misunderstanding. I am in favour of writing books on the Resistance. Even the prejudiced and ill-intentioned ones have some truth in them. In my paper I explained that, even in many official documents, facts are purposely mis-represented in order to conceal intentions and actions unsuitable or harmful to the cause, or to promote political aims still in the future. To-day, when many of the documents from the secret archives of the Foreign Office have been published, not many can doubt the hostile activities of the British officers who at that time led the campaign against EAM-ELAS in the mountains of Greece. But there are others too who have criticised and slandered the National Liberation movement and some "leftists" have gone so far as to describe ELAS as a "British unit". I am of the opinion that nothing should be hidden. We of EAM-ELAS have a duty to speak openly and freely, to tell people the truth both about our successes and about our mistakes and defects. Otherwise our enemies will seize on some actual mistake and interpret it in accordance with their interests. This is what I was trying to do in my talk.

Vasilis Pesmazoglou: If I understood the speech correctly, the basic problem was a lack of communication between the leadership and the rank-and-file, as a consequence of which a mistake was made and EAM-ELAS capitulated. I am raising two points; 1) If they had not gone to the Lebanon and had not capitulated, what do you think would have been the outcome given the world context? and 2) Do you think this lack of contact an adequate explanation of the mistake?

Thanasis Hajis: It is true there was a lack of regular communication between the leadership and the rank-and-file in KKE and EAM. The leadership had become cut off from the movement and from the people. But it is also true that all the organisations, from the highest to the lowest, struggled throughout the Occupation in the belief that national liberation was the necessary condition for the satisfactory settlement of all the unsolved political and social problems of our country which constituted EAM's ultimate aim. This was EAM's line and this its spirit. But tactics, the actual road to be followed, was not the same for the leadership and for the rank-and-file of the popular movement. Finally, it was the leadership's tactics which prevailed. Thus, when the leadership, despite persistent rank-and-file opposition, accepted the Lebanon agreement, sent ministers to participate in the bourgeois government-in-exile and signed the Caserta Agreement, the rank-and-file, possessed by revolutionary fervour, did not understand the change which had occurred and believed that the leadership was manoeuvring in order to achieve a more effective victory at the cost of fewer sacrifices by neutralising British and reactionary intrigues. It

---

* Mr. Hajis contributed to the discussion in Greek and his contributions were relayed to the audience in simultaneous translation. Under these circumstances it is natural that he felt the need to carry out a revision of the text.

did not realise that the leadership had lost its way and was following its own line, a line of capitulation. This was the majority line within the Political Bureau of the KKE Central Committee. It had made its choice for a smooth passage from Occupation to freedom. It regarded such a course as dictated by the Allied line, allegedly a line of co-operation between the Soviet Union and the Western powers — Britain and the US — which would continue for many years after the war. In other words it regarded this co-operation as "the alliance of the century". This mistaken viewpoint brought the leadership into opposition with the rank-and-file which was continuing the revolutionary struggle for liberation and popular democracy*. The strange thing was that the leadership did not obstruct the movement's triumphant progress. This was because it considered that the expansion of the movement lent it more authority and negotiating muscle both inside and outside the "national" government. Thus it came about that the struggle failed though there were no forces within Greece to withstand the popular revolutionary movement and the British only disposed of a minimal military force — Lord Jellicoe's — and a few British Military Mission officers scattered about the country.

If EAM-ELAS had taken power in October 1944 — which it could have taken unopposed — and had gone on to co-operate with the popular democratic movements in the other Balkan countries which had established their own People's Democracies, a British armed intervention would have been difficult if not impossible. Even if we take the most pessimistic view, that the British would have decided to intervene militarily and would have been successful, the popular revolutionary movement should still have taken power in October. It should not have voluntarily handed over power to the bankrupt bourgeoisie and let itself be transformed — as it did — into a tool for the re-establishment of a state of violence, exploitation and subservience to Anglo-American imperialism. When power is to be had for the asking and a revolutionary movement has the ability to take it and does not do so, then that movement has ceased to be revolutionary and will inevitably face defeat, destruction and dissolution.

Vasilis Pesmazoglou: Regarding the alliance with the USSR, what documents are there to show that this opinion existed in KKE throughout this period? — that the alliance would continue? How did they explain the favourable stand of the British Military Mission towards EDES and EKKA in the mountains?

Thanasis Hajis: The first time the viewpoint that the alliance between the USSR and the Western Powers was a long-term one and would last until the complete elimination of fascism was expounded in the KKE

---

* The concept of *laïki dimokratia* is nowhere officially defined. It was a broad programme of popular participation, a degree of public ownership and extended social welfare, not unlike the British Labour programme of 1945.

RESISTANCE OR NATIONAL LIBERATION MOVEMENT?

Central Committee was at its meeting on the dissolution of the Comintern. This viewpoint determined the leadership's insistence on the achievement of "national unity" with the leaders of the bourgeois parties, a unity which was never achieved and which it was not even possible to achieve.

Chris Carratt: Was Siantos angry with Rousos when he came back from the Lebanon and had signed the agreement with Papandreou?

Thanasis Hajis: Of course he was angry, just as all the members and followers of the EAM movement were angry. The Lebanon Agreement was unanimously condemned by the National Council*, by all EAM-ELAS organisations and by KKE. Siantos was right to be angry because Rousos had violated all the terms of reference given him when he left for the Middle East with the popular movement's delegation.

Question from the auditorium: Mr. Hajis said that, in saying "NO" to the Italians, Metaxas had secured the interests of the Greek bourgeoisie with the British. Is there evidence, are there documents?

Thanasis Hajis: Yes. There is evidence such as the pre-war statement by Metaxas that the frontiers of Greece are the British Empire's line of defence.

The previous questioner: In view of the fact that it had the support of 85%-90% of the population, why did not EAM-ELAS contest the 1946 elections?

Thanasis Hajis: At the February 1946 session of the Central Committee it was actually decided to take part in the elections, since there were parliamentary illusions. But Zachariadis thought the situation was revolutionary and did not want to get entangled in parliamentary procedures. He thought that this would alienate people from the prospect of an armed confrontation which they wanted and at the same time block that prospect. I think this was a great mistake. Many documents show that the majority of our party organisers in the regions favoured participating in elections.

The next question, almost incomprehensible on the tape-recording, appeared to repeat the first one on self-criticism and lack of communication, expanding into differences between socialism and social democracy and was cut short by the Chairman.

Thanasis Hajis: These arguments could be debated but they do not take into account one important consideration. When EAM-ELAS went to the Lebanon to negotiate, it already had its own government PEEA and a National Council which was the elected parliament of Greece. The people had expressed its will — that we do not need to unite with those who deserted the country, with the forces which directly or indirectly attack the national liberation movement when they do not openly collaborate with the Occupation. But the leadership overesti-

---

* the elected parliament of liberated Greece, *see* below

mated the power of the British and underestimated that of the people. As a result of this miscalculation, the leadership capitulated.

Question from the auditorium: On the role of the USSR: 1) Do you think that capitulation to the British was in any way the result of direct or indirect pressure brought to bear by the Soviet Military Mission? and 2) Given what secret understandings might have existed between the Soviets and the British, do you think that the Soviet Union could have played a more constructive role in guiding the Greek leadership to avoid mistakes?

Thanasis Hajis: Throughout the occupation we had no contact with the Soviet Union, not even through Tito until June 1944 when Tzimas went to Yugoslavia. The Soviet Military Mission which arrived at ELAS GHQ at the end of August 1944 was a team whose task was to collect military information and was expressly forbidden by the Red Army High Command from intervening in Greek political affairs. Concrete official evidence for the existence of an Anglo-Soviet agreement assigning Greece to the British sphere of influence does not exist or at least has not been published. The KKE & EAM leadership had much evidence which showed that the Soviet Union, because of her own difficulties, could not contribute immediate active assistance to the Greek national liberation movement. We also knew that she had always feared a separate alliance between the US, Great Britain and Germany. She was very careful not to provoke any such agreement. We communists wanted to guess what Soviet interests were in order to act in accordance with them. But unfortunately we guessed wrong and did things which made it very difficult for the USSR to act in favour of us.

George Alexander: Mr Hajis said that at the top level of the leadership there were people who believed that the alliance would persist after the war. Will he please name these people and explain why they opposed Rousos when he signed the agreement?

Thanasis Hajis: As I have already said, there were two tendencies in the KKE leadership. One — the majority — believed that the alliance between the USSR, the US and Great Britian would continue after the war and that, in the Greek context, this meant collaboration with the other political parties. The minority view was that this alliance was adapted to circumstances and therefore just a temporary one, that there was even a danger of the alliance breaking up during the war, and that the British were fighting the Germans as their competitors and not as fascists. It was a repeat of World War I — they were fighting to maintain the power and control they had acquired then. Since there was such a possibility of the British joining the Germans against the Soviet Union, an alliance which would have inevitably turned against the revolutionary popular movements, KKE and EAM should have prepared to face such a threat. The Party and the movement foresaw this danger. Many "signals" had reached the leadership from the rank-and-file. But the leadership saw nothing.

George Alexander: Would the speaker please name them?
Thanasis Hajis: Siantos, Zevgos, Plumbidis and Anastasiadis, all members of the Political Bureau, agreed with our rank-and-file and with the people, as did the majority of the KKE and EAM cadres who worked in the regional organisations and in the higher ELAS commands. But at the critical moment they were not able to prevail.
Question from the auditorium: Since Mr. Hajis was the one who resisted Zachariadis' opinion on the elections at the conference, why did he not resist the telegram sent to him by Zachariadis to Salonica where he had gone to prepare for the elections as organiser for Macedonia?
Thanasis Hajis: Anybody who knows how communist parties function *(Laughter)* will know why a small faction could not come out in opposition against the rest of the Party which followed the instructions of its leadership.

The Battle of Athens and the role of the British

Heinz Richter

The events of December 1944, which have become known in history as *The Dekemvriana,* represent the decisive turning point in Greece's contemporary history. The term *Dekemvriana* denotes the armed clash between Greek and British armed forces and units of the National Liberation Army (ELAS) in Athens. The conflict started on 3 December when Greek policemen fired at unarmed EAM demonstrators, and ended on 11 January 1945 with the conclusion of an armistice. On 12 February peace came about with the signing of the Varkiza Agreement.

Between these barren dates, one of the most tragic chapters of Greek history occurred. The military defeat of a part of ELAS in the battle of Athens represents the anticlimax to its former indisputable military successes against the Axis occupiers. However important ELAS' military activities were for the development of the South-east European war theatre, for Greece the fact that ELAS had liberated most of Greece by October 1944 had a much greater significance, a political one. In the freed areas a new social and political order was created by the grassroots of society. Its structures differed radically from the traditional ones. The main features of the prewar state had been oligarchical rule, clientelism, *"rousfetism"** and centralism. By contrast the new order was characterized by factors such as selfgovernment, people's rights, voting, equality of women, decentralization to mention only a few. In brief, thanks to the Resistance Movement, a fundamental change of the Greek state was now within view.

The military defeat of ELAS in December 1944 brought this development to an abrupt end. In the months that followed the Varkiza Agreement, a counter-revolutionary tide hit Greece sweeping away everything the Resistance had built up and brought back to the surface the old structures that still trouble Greece. During the Occupation the labour unions had been united into one powerful federation. After Varkiza they fell again under the influence of the state which splintered the federation into 1,500 small unions engulfed in party strifes. The army likewise was purged of all liberal and leftist elements and came

---

* The Greek system of nepotism and patronage.

under the control of an extreme right wing secret organization (IDEA) — of which a "notable" later member was George Papadopoulos.* The police and state machinery were not purged of the fascist elements and collaborators as provided for in the Varkiza Agreement, but of the progressive elements. In Greece the collaborators were not punished as in the other European countries but rather rewarded for their former "anti-communist" services. The economic and political oligarchy returned to power. The former resistance fighters were thrown into prisons by the thousand and persecuted for the most trifling reasons. Simultaneously a private power apparatus of the extreme Right came into being and successfully competed with the Greek state; this is what the Greeks call *parakratos*. The Civil War was caused much more by desperation and hopelessness resulting from the White Terror than by the alleged Communist drive to power.

The list of these negative consequences in the aftermath of the *Dekemvriana* which are still felt today might be much longer. The few points that have been stressed may depict the great significance that the *Dekemvriana* have for Greek history. Likewise it becomes obvious that the after-effects of the *Dekemvriana* had a significance which goes far beyond the Greek borders. They affected the whole post-war history of the Balkans if not of Europe. The *Dekemvriana* for this reason take on an importance extending beyond mere academic interest and requiring a detailed analysis. But this task goes beyond the scope of my exposition and the time-limit available. So I will only deal with three questions raised by this complicated problem which I will try to answer.

1. What was the nature of the *Dekemvriana*?
2. Who was ultimately responsible for their outbreak?
3. Could the *Dekemvriana* have been avoided?

The question on the nature of the *Dekemvriana* was first answered by Prime Minister Churchill himself. On 8 January 1945 he stated before the House of Commons that 'there was... a fairly well organized plot or plan by which ELAS should march down upon Athens and seize it by armed force'. Even at the time this plot-to-seize-power theory was met with strong scepticism in Great Britain and the USA The British press from the leftist *New Statesman* to the conservative *Times* were unanimous in refuting this plot thesis. It was likewise criticized in the House of Commons not only by leftists like the labourite Aneurin Bevan and the communist William Gallacher but also by the leaders of the Liberal Party, Sir Percy Harris, and of the Labour Party, Arthur Greenwood. In the USA criticism was not confined to the press. President Roosevelt himself was appalled and the Secretary of State Stettinius denounced British intervention publicly. Two years later, how-

---

* The leader of the military Junta which carried out the *coup* of April 1967 and head of the dictatorial government from that date till November 1973.

ever, at the beginning of the Cold War, the Churchill thesis prevailed. Not only news-commentators and journalists, but also historians of the stature of William Hardy McNeill accepted Churchill's view. From then on writers and historians alike repeated this theory even more enthusiastically and over and over again. Two recent examples are George Kousoulas and Henry Maule. According to the views of these writers Churchill's unselfish intervention saved Greece from falling under the dictatorship of the proletariat. This point of view has been repeatedly and thoroughly exploited and has become almost a political creed.

The constant repetition of this plot-to-seize-power theory has until very recently obscured the fact that there had from very early been dissenting voices. As early as 1949 Stavrianos had doubted this theory in an article written for the *American Slavic and East European Review* and in 1952 he convincingly proved in his book 'Greece: American Dilemma and Opportunity' that Churchill's theory belonged to the realm of myth. The first professional historian who after a pause of 20 years reviewed the events of December 1944 critically was John Iatridis in his book 'Revolt in Athens. The Greek Communist Second Round' which appeared in 1972. He stated flatly:

'However great KKE's role in the upheaval was, to see the entire affair as the product of a deliberate Communist decision to seize power by force is to fail to recognize the deeper roots of the conflict. The real causes must be sought in the economic, social, political, and psychological exhaustion inherited from the past and aggravated by the war, foreign occupation, and external manipulation'. Accordingly Iatridis does not see "genuine villains" in this Greek drama, but 'a repletion with human errors'. In his opinion even KKE was the 'victim of a general malaise and of a climate conducive to violence to which it had contributed'. He considers the *Dekemvriana* the result of the conflict of two different concepts of society and of a profound mutual mistrust which made a peaceful solution impossible. For him the outbreak of actual fighting is the climax of a process of escalation which had acquired a momentum of its own, got out of control and led inexorably to civil war.' Only cool reason, the rarest of diplomatic skills, and the most profound devotion to the welfare of the entire nation could have reversed this disastrous course'. He includes British policy towards Greece in this argument, its main mistake having been its inconsistency. Iatridis mentions certain erroneous decisions of Churchill but he subordinates them to his main thesis of sliding or stumbling into the war, a thesis which is subject to the same problems as Lloyd George's almost identical one about the outbreak of the First World War. From this point of view nobody was responsible for the outbreak of the *Dekemvriana* which becomes a mere stroke of fate or a regrettable error of history.

At about the same time the present speaker analysed these events within the framework of a wider study on the history of Greece in the decade from 1936 to 1946.* He arrived at the following thesis and conclusions: The *Dekemvriana* were by no means a previously prepared Communist revolution. In December 1944 the alternatives did not read dictatorship of the proletariat or liberal democracy, but national independence, people's sovereignty and democratic socialism or foreign tutelage and oligarchical rule. The *Dekemvriana* was the intervention which Churchill had prepared with all diplomatic and military diligence since 1943 in order to destroy the entire Greek Resistance Movement and to re-establish the pre-war semi-colonial dependency. The intervention in Greece was a part of the policy to re-establish the Empire, to safeguard its lines of communication and to erect an anticommunist bulwark against the Soviet Union. They were an element of the spheres-of-interest policy the rules of which the British Ambassador in Greece Sir Edmund Lyons had phrased in 1841 and which were still considered valid in 1944: 'A Greece truly independent is an absurdity. Greece is Russian or she is English; and since she must not be Russian it is necessary that she be English'. The Greek monarchs were traditionally supposed to be guarantors of Greece's pro-British policy. Hence Churchill fought for the restoration of George II to the Greek throne. But not even George II was the decisive factor. The decisive factor was Churchill's extreme dislike of social change. There is no doubt that Churchill within the limitations of his class was a good democrat – at home; but abroad was a different matter. To what extent this policy was influenced by financial interests of the City we do not know precisely, but we cannot exclude them. Thus the *Dekemvriana* was an intervention to re-establish the *status quo ante*.

Besides this aspect of the *Dekemvriana* which was determined by foreign factors there was a domestic Greek equivalent which was closely related to the former through the person of the King. On the surface this domestic aspect was determined by the antagonism between monarchy and republic; in reality the whole social and political system was at stake. The Greek monarchy had discredited itself by its active participation in the fascist dictatorship of Metaxas and there was a consensus of all political forces except for a few fanatical royalists and fascists – both of whom futher compromised the cause of the King by collaboration – that the post-war state would be a republic. But the Republicans had neither a common organization nor did they agree on the post-war political and social order. True, the old politicians demanded the republic but under their oligarchical rule and they therefore did not join the Resistance Movement. The Resistance was split into various organizations with various rather vague political programmes for the post-war system. The end of this confusion was brought about

---

* Heinz Richter: 'Griechenland zwischen Revolution und Konterrevolution (1936-1946)' *Frankfurt*, 1973, also in Greek translation: '1936-1946 Dyo Epanastaseis kai Antepanastaseis stin Ellada.' 2v. Exantas. *Athens*, 1975.

by the model which EAM put into practice in the liberated areas, which, as we have already mentioned, heralded the birth of a new social and political order from the grassroots. It is true, the Greek communists played a major role in this development but the danger of a communist takeover was non-existent. In contrast to Tito, KKE adhered formalistically to the orthodox prescriptions for revolution and these prescribed the establishment of bourgeois democracy for Greece. Quite on the contrary, KKE considered some of the radical democratic reforms initiated by EAM-ELAS with deep mistrust and called to order all those who tried to accelerate the process of social transformation. Particularly it opposed all activities which might result in a conflict with Great Britain. The internal characteristics of the post-war state erected on this basis would have been liberalism, democracy and social reform. Its foreign relations with Great Britain would have been characterized by equal partnership.

This development endangered the position of the Greek oligarchy. Already during the Occupation the right-wing collaborating faction began to "defend" its position under the disguise of crusading against Communism. It is true that the liberal and republican faction continued to struggle for the cause of the republic but it was increasingly afraid of the communist danger which foreign propaganda whispered to it. Finally, the *Dekemvriana* represents the open Civil War of the extreme Right against the progressive Left. Simultaneously this civil war served as a proof *post eventum* of the alleged earlier existence of the communist danger and contributed to reunify the bourgeois camp.

From this point of view the *Dekemvriana* take on a double character. They are simultaneously a domestic civil strife and a foreign intervention. Only this twofold character can explain certain of the events. For instance, without the fact that the *Dekemvriana* was a civil war as well, we cannot understand the terrible outrages from both sides. If we take the civil war character into consideration the whole discussion which side committed more crimes becomes irrelevant because such things are integral parts of every civil war. The decisive question boils down to this: which side pushed developments over the line where discussion and compromise were still possible?

The simplest and most non-controversial answer would be: it was that anonymous group of policemen. It is true that they fired the first shots during the *Dekemvriana,* but was that really the point of no return? We do not think so. The crucial day was not 3 December but rather the 5th: After the events of 3 December the Greek party leaders had started talks concerning a change of government. For some time Archbishop Damaskinos was named as a possible new prime minister. At noon on 4 December Ambassador Leeper informed the Foreign Office: 'Since yesterday's events, I am more strongly of the opinion that Papandreou cannot carry on; the Government must be strongly reinforced so that the nation may be given greater confidence under such a Government... it may even be possible... to summon a conference with the Left in an effort to stop civil war.' In the evening of the same day the talks of the Greek party leaders ended successfully. The leader of the Liberal party, Themistocles Sofoulis, was to become the new prime minister. Leeper recommended that London try a new start with Sofoulis.

Indeed this solution would have made possible a new start and would have opened the way for a peaceful solution of the crisis. The Liberals appreciated the Left's desire for security guarantees and so Sofoulis would certainly have found a mutually acceptable compromise on the disarmament question. The Left supported this solution. After all its ministers had resigned on 1 December in order to clear the way towards this solution. When Papandreou telegraphed his resignation from the premiership to London on the afternoon of 4 December a last chance to de-escalate the crisis, literally in the last minute, had become reality. In London Churchill had observed developments by means of the incoming telegrams from Athens until late in the night. In his memoirs he recalls the decisive minutes 'Anthony (Eden) and I were together till about two o'clock, and were entirely agreed that we must open fire. Seeing how tired he was, I said to him, "If you like to go to bed, leave it to me". He did.' Some moments later Churchill drafted the two decisive instructions, which pushed the matter beyond the point of no return.

The first telegram he directed to Leeper not to Scobie as he states in his memoirs. This fact is easily proved by the original which is in the Public Record Office. Churchill sent the following instructions: 'This is not time to dabble in Greek politics or to imagine that Geek politicians of varying shades can affect the situation. You should not worry about Greek Government compositions. The matter is one of life and death. You must force (in his memoirs it is "urge") Papandreou to stand to his duty and assure him he will be supported by all our forces if he does so. (The next two sentences are missing in Churchill's memoirs) Should he resign, he should be locked up till he comes to his senses, when the fighting will probably be over. It might be that he should be in bed and inaccessible. The day has long gone past when any particular group of Greek politicians can influence this mob rising. His only chance is to come through with us . . .'.*

Five minutes later Churchill sent the notorious 'Don't hesitate to fire', telegram to General Scobie. In Athens Papandreou obediently withdrew his resignation and Sofoulis protested in vain against this high-handed treatment. The die was cast, compromise was no longer possible. One question is posed here: was Churchill's decision a spontaneous reaction, perhaps a sort of Gordian knot solution to the crisis or was it just the final result of a process which had been decided on

---

* Prime Minister to Mr. Leeper 5 December 1944 R 19.933/745/19

long before? We mentioned at the beginning of this exposition that Churchill had been preparing for intervention since 1943. The limited time available makes it impossible to describe all the steps of this process but we will try to mention the most important ones. At the same time we can observe a fascinating coincidence: whenever Churchill moved one step further towards confrontation warning voices were heard predicting the final outbreak of civil war. Unfortunately no one paid attention.

The dominating factor was the question of George II's return to Greece. To Churchill this question was one-dimensional. He considered George II as the legitimate head of the Greek state, as a loyal ally who had to be restored to his throne. Churchill did not recognize that the antagonism between monarchy and republic was no longer the traditional conflict within the Greek bourgeoisie, a conflict which had determined political developments between the First World War and the Metaxas dictatorship, but that it had taken on a new dimension. Churchill did not understand that in Greece a new popular movement had come into being born out of the Resistance. Churchill considered the Greek Resistance Movement a mere military enterprise to fight the Germans and did not see that it had become a dynamic political force which he could not activate or de-activate whenever it pleased him. The question which must be put here is: did Churchill really not understand this or did he not want to? Churchill rarely received objective reports on the real character and purposes of the Greek Resistance. Most of his information came from Foreign Office channels reflecting traditional bias and pre-conceptions about Greek pre-war politics. Therefore Churchill considered the Resistance leaders as miserable banditti or communist troublemakers who — if necessary — could be brought to reason by a little show of strength. In other words, Churchill did not comprehend the true character of the Greek Resistance Movement as a broad popular movement which included all strata of society and in which the communists played an important but not a decisive, dominating role. As he under-estimated EAM's strength he refused to take a clear public stand on the constitutional issue. The result was that the Greek Left was under the impression that it was British policy to restore the pre-war regime. The conflict was programmed.

There had been warnings. The first came as early as April 1943 from Brigadier Myers, who warned that there would be a civil war if the Greek king should return without a plebiscite. In order to avoid this it was necessary for the British government to declare that they had no intention to impose the King by force. On 2 October 1943 Myers repeated his warnings to Churchill himself and tried to make him change British policy but to no avail. The net result was increased hostilities of the Foreign Office towards him. Myers was not allowed to return to Greece. Churchill stuck to his decision of 29 September

1943 to use force in Greece. The next important step towards conflict was the means by which Churchill suppressed the unrest in the Greek armed forces in spring 1944. Political demonstrations among the forces were interpreted as mutiny and after its suppression the Greek armed forces were purged of all Leftists and Republicans and became staunchly royalist and anti-communist. The nomination of Papandreou as the new prime minister, the way in which Leeper manipulated the Lebanon conference from behind the scenes and the three months' spheres of interest agreement with the Soviets represent the next steps. A further decisive step was taken during a meeting of the War Cabinet in July 1944.

Among the documents before that meeting was the report of the liaison officer Major Bathgate on the Greek guerrilla movement. Unfortunately this report is not to be found in the Public Record Office. By chance I found portions of it in the archives of the Trades Union Congress. One paragraph is of particular interest. Major Bathgate wrote: 'We owe a debt to Greece over the whole *Andarte** movement, and it is in our interests and morally binding upon us, to scrap the whole affair when the Germans are driven out. This can only be done by British troops and a few young and very active Greek commanders'. In other words, Major Bathgate proposed that, when the Germans left the country, the British government should start a war in order to destroy the Greek Resistance Movements by British arms.

This incredible recommendation induced a labourite TUC politician in a high position (he had access to Cabinet papers), whose identity I have not yet been able to establish, to write a memorandum entitled "Greek Policy — A New Start" and submit it to the War Cabinet. This paper was also obtained from the TUC archives.

This memorandum analyses the reasons which had led to the crisis of Greek politics in summer 1944. Its author considered two points, which had been decisively influenced by British policy, to be of prime importance: the question of the restoration of the Greek king and the policy of dissolving ELAS. The author of the memorandum put forward observations which cannot be dealt with due to lack of time but which correspond with those I have made, especially those pertaining to the character of EAM. Then he presented concrete suggestions for a new British policy towards Greece. I wish to mention a few:

'King George and Papandreou should be induced to make declarations which will settle the constitutional issue for good and all. . . HMG should then make some comment on these declarations which will show that, while the issue involved is one for the Greeks themselves to settle, the declarations have our full good will. The denunciations of EAM should be scrupulously avoided, and everything possible should be said and done to show that, if EAM will behave like a demo-

---

* The Greek word for guerrilla, *lit.* rebel.

cratic, national movement HMG will treat it as such. The formula for this will not be easy to find, but in general they must be variants of the theme. 'Let bygones by bygones'. . . We should make it plain to Papandreou that HMG will give him no support in any attempt to divide the leaders of EAM or split or dissolve ELAS. HMG should do what can be done to strengthen the position of Svolos and other democratic leaders in EAM and to encourage democratic officers to join ELAS. . . . If there is to be a Greek Government at all, it should be made fully responsible for its own decisions, and Greeks, inside and outside Greece, should be disabused of the view, now so widely held, that we want to run the policy of the Greek government for them. We should at once remove from Greece all BLOs* of the Major Bathgate class. We should persuade Papandreou to make another supreme attempt, not to dissolve any of the guerrilla forces, but to unify their efforts under a common leadership. Much the best way of doing this would be to find some officer of high prestige to take command both of the Brigades outside Greece, and of the guerrillas within. I can only think of one man who would have enough authority to succeed – General Plastiras. We should dismiss from our minds any idea that HMG can "restore order" or "liquidate the guerrillas" after the war. The idea could only arise in a mind as ignorant and prejudiced as Major Bathgate's. But if the Greeks come to know that anyone had even talked of it, great and lasting harm might be done.'

Indeed, these suggestions would have rendered a new start possible and they would in all probability have prevented the *Dekemvriana*. Unfortunately the author's suggestions fell on deaf ears and the crisis continued to escalate. The next two steps were the Caserta Agreement and the notorious percentage agreement at Moscow in October 1944 by which, as we have recently learned, spheres of interest without any time limit were created. Who would be surprised that the last warnings of people like the Resistance politician Petimezas** ("Our task is to avoid civil war at all costs") were not heeded? Until the bitter end the Greek Left tried to avoid civil war as is proved by its constant readiness to compromise which came close to self-abnegation. Churchill on the other hand was not interested in compromises, he wanted the unconditional surrender of the Greek Left and as this was not offered he sought conflict. How determined Churchill's course was is proved by his instructions to Leeper of 30 November: 'It is important to let it be known that if there is a civil war in Greece we shall be on the side of the Government. . . and above all that we shall not hesitate to shoot'.† We can with great certainty assume that this message was

---

* British Liaison Officers.
** Report on Greek Political Situation submitted to GHQ. ME by Mr Petimezas November 1944 R21. 462/475/19
† Prime Minister's Personal Minute Serial No. M1166/4, 30 M.44 R19. 341/745/19

passed on to Papandreou and thus indirectly influenced the decision of those policemen to open fire on the unarmed demonstrators.

Without Churchill's support the Greek Right would never have dared to start a civil war against the Left. Thus the ultimate responsibility for the *Dekemvriana* rests with Churchill. But this was only one side of British policy towards Greece, there were on the other hand many important dissenting voices which advocated a totally different course which would certainly have led to a peaceful solution. This must be put on the record of history as well. It is the tragedy of Anglo-Greek relations that these voices did not prevail.

DISCUSSION

A commentator from the auditorium (John Ryan?) said that the document referred to as showing the reason why the British were scared of the Greek people is in the Public Record Office.

Heinz Richter: As I said, I didn't find this document in the Public Record Office but at the TUC. What is more important is the analysis accompanying it. For me, it is important that there were at that time such documents, such suggestions. Major Bathgate himself was not so important. But you see I noticed another thing: that the information reaching the FO and Churchill came from people like Major Bathgate. To give another example, from 1945: in a village near Salonica there was an outrage against the Left. The newspapers wrote of it the other way round. So did the British Consul in his report to his superiors. When he was asked about this, he said "Let other people do propaganda for the Left. I won't." It is exactly there that we have the main point.

George Alexander: It seems to me that the substance of what you said is that the British provoked the December events because Sofoulis, the leading Liberal, might have been able to reach an acceptable agreement with EAM-ELAS (on the demobilisation issue.) If this is so, I would like to know why did Sofoulis refuse to accept the demobilisation decree formulated by the Papandreou government, that there should be a unit formed of equal ELAS and EDES components?

Heinz Richter: Probably for the same reason that ELAS refused it. EAM-ELAS was ready to agree to equal strength but *really* equal strength. They did not want separate units but units integrated down to the battle-group. Otherwise the ELAS force could be sent to the North, to "defend the borders against Tito", whilst a *coup d'état* was carried out in Athens.

George Alexander: Lovely! Why didn't Sofoulis accept Papandreou's decree?

Heinz Richter: To which stage are you referring? When? Sofoulis, as far as I know was not included in the discussion.

Interruption from the auditorium: What do you mean? What date?
George Alexander: On 28 November.
Heinz Richter: I have not heard that Sofoulis was at the talks then.
George Alexander: Haven't you consulted the telegrams in the Public Record Office?
Heinz Richter: Some of them.
George Alexander: Sofoulis was sitting there with Leeper in the Embassy refusing to sign Papandreou's decree.
Heinz Richter: But you know as well as I do that Sofoulis pursued a policy sometimes this way sometimes that way. In 1945 remember, when he took over the premiership, he arranged the elections and, afterwards, when he resigned, he said 'Unfortunately they were not conducted in the proper way.'
George Alexander: On 5 December, Churchill refused to allow Sofoulis to become premier and if he had become premier he could have reached an agreement with ELAS on the demobilisation issue?
Heinz Richter: Certainly...
George Alexander (interrupting): And yet, on 28 November, he refused to accept Papandreou's settlement?
Heinz Richter: It is no use insisting on this particular document. If you would be kind enough to give or send it to me so that I can read it... At the moment we are playing with cards I don't know.
B. Sweet-Escott: I want to make a point — I think a rather important one. You mentioned the influence of the City as an important element in the formation of British policy, and I am tired of reading this in books on Greece. I've been in the City for 40 years in all, except during wartime and all I know of City interests in Athens does not really amount to a peanut. There was of course Hambro's Bank which issued loans on behalf of the Greek Government but it didn't do this to influence British policy and it was the British who mainly suffered when the loans were in default. Much the most important were the Athens, Piraeus and Phaleron Power Stations and the Athens buses and trams all owned by the Pearson (Lord Cowdray's) Group since 1930. They were sold in the 70's for about £20m. Then there was the Lake Copais Company which had drained a lake in Boeotia and now farmed directly or let out 100 sq. miles of very fertile territory. That was sold early in the 50's for just under £2m. There was also the Ionian Bank founded in 1839 to be the bank of issue of the Ionian Islands when they were part of the British Empire. After they were given to Greece in 1863, it expanded to Athens, Egypt and Cyprus and elsewhere and bought another Greek bank, the Popular. This bank and the Ionian's Greek branches were sold in 1957 for just under £700,000. Hardly peanuts I suppose, as I said, but when you take it all together the British interests were a fraction of what they were in Iran or Egypt. I think the importance of the City in the formation of British policy was not very considerable.

Heinz Richter: Well, there is no document to prove British interests directly. But we must take into account: 1) that a third of the Greek Budget went on servicing former British loans, even in 1945: if the Greeks had any money, then they had to pay up. It was not the British government — certainly not. But a national economy does not exist in a vacuum. History has proved — even in my own country — that the embassies are sometimes the best local salesmen for a national economy. And 2) that the Bank of Greece was controlled by some families of the Greek financial oligarchy and to a certain degree by some British banks. I don't know which, but shares were held by British banks. It is a possibility we must not forget because we had a similar state of affairs under the Junta — ESSO, Tom Pappas, etc.

E.H. Cookridge: We can probably accept most of what you said about Churchill's discussions and decisions but you only mentioned Leeper in passing. Surely Churchill took his decisions mainly on the basis of reports from Leeper and I would like to ask your opinion about Leeper's reports, remembering that, in August 1943 and even earlier, before he was ambassador, when he was political adviser to Casey* and a member of the Political Warfare Executive, Leeper acted very much on his own and even in divergence from the FO and SIS. Very early in the war one SIS report said that the broad Left had an estimated support of 40% and the royalists 2%. In his own book,** Leeper repeats again and again that he acted on instructions. Is it your opinion that this is whitewash, that he wanted to gloss over his own interventions?

Heinz Richter: One of Leeper's main characteristics was his inconsistency. Whenever he was left alone and thus had the chance for a sober analysis of the situation, his conclusions and suggestions were rather objective and close to reality, *e.g.* when he became ambassador to the Greek Government-in-exile his first account of Greek politics was rather good, as is proved by his memoirs ('The Foreign Office was speaking with two voices'). Again, in April 1945 when Leeper became *de facto* "High Commissioner" for Greece, then he developed a wonderful scheme how this "High Commission" should function; and then there was exactly the same story as before. When Churchill received this plan he sent furious telegrams — typical ones — and told Leeper: 'You must not go into the details of Greek policy'. The result: Leeper shrunk back. There had been the same story in August 1943. First, he was enthusiastic about the Resistance delegation. This was a chance. But, when those telegrams came from Churchill, he changed. There was another fantastic example when Labour came to power. Then he again started an initiative. But, as soon as he received instructions, he shrank back and just carried them out obediently: Leeper may thus be characterised as a well-functioning tool of the FO.

---

* The late Rt. Hon. R.G. Casey, Minister of State for the Middle East.
** 'When Greek meets Greek'. Chatto and Windus, *London,* 1950.

Markos Dragoumis (Press Councillor, Greek Embassy): I refer to the move Churchill made on Christmas Eve when he offered terms to ELAS which were rejected. These terms were much better than those ELAS got at Varkiza. How does this fit with your theory of Churchill's total instransigence and the total willingness of the other side to compromise?

Heinz Richter: The conference at Christmas 1944 was a political showpiece. The real decision had been made on the previous evening when Churchill met Damaskinos aboard the Ajax and suddenly discovered that he was not a communist or a collaborator but that he was a staunch anti-communist. Then he decided "O.K. Let's take him".

Markos Dragoumis: If the conference was a showpiece why did Churchill go to it? Why did he go to Athens at all?

Heinz Richter: Criticism had become too strong, even in the House of Commons. In his memoirs he says there were only 30 votes against him but he does not say that there were more than 200 abstentions. He simply had to find a political solution. There would have been a unique chance if Churchill had met the EAM-ELAS leaders and had discovered that they were not what he thought. The offers which he made must not be taken seriously. If he had met the EAM-ELAS leaders, the armistice dealings could then have been concluded much earlier.

Markos Dragoumis: But did he not offer terms much better than ELAS got in the end?

Heinz Richter: He did not offer any terms. If you read the proceedings, you have Churchill's introductory remarks — words without much content; then the discussion started, next day it continued, and, finally, when Siantos tabled his suggestions, the whole thing was blocked. 24 December, as I see it, was a bid to re-unify the bourgeois camp — nothing more.

The Don Stott Affair: Overtures for an Anglo-German local peace in Greece

Hagen Fleischer

There are various reasons for my decision to choose this topic. Basically it was due to the still unsolved controversy, namely whether the strange talks of a New Zealand officer with high German authorities in occupied Athens represented merely an adventurous but unconnected "war story" or — as usually claimed — 'one of the greatest treacheries practised by British imperialism against the peoples and particularly against the Greek people during World War II'.[1]

The last version serves not only to demonstrate the suspected British anti-soviet machinations, but the so-called "Don Stott Mission" is also supposed to be the main impulse for the foundation of the collaborating "Security Battalions" — in reality founded previously; it is likewise alleged as one of the causes provoking civil war between the two greatest guerrilla organizations, EDES and ELAS, — a civil war which had already broken out some weeks before. The "Mission" has finally been quoted as the decisive factor for far-reaching subsequent events like the takeover of the premiership by George Papandreou.[2] On the other hand, real and important consequences of this complicated affair have been overlooked.

This study aims at the elucidation of the hidden points — based mainly on unpublished and as yet unknown sources in British, German and Greek archives, since the scarcity of established knowledge so far allowed large-scale speculations.

In May 1941 Sergeant Donald John Stott had been wounded and captured in Crete but soon managed to escape — together with his close friend Bob Morton — from a German prison camp by pole-vaulting the barbed wire in broad daylight. After several months in hiding and after some abortive attempts at sailing to the Middle East they finally reached Alexandria. There both joined the SOE and repeatedly smuggled out Allied prisoners from Crete by submarine. After an unsuccessful sabotage operation in North Africa Stott, already a lieutenant, was parachuted back into Greece in April 1943. In June he was the "chief hero" of the destruction of the Asopos viaduct[3], interrupting thereby the only north-south railway line through Greece for 71 days.

Some weeks later Stott had been appointed liaison officer with

ELAS with his headquarters in Attica and Boeotia. Although the captain undoubtedly holds conservative views, he maintains tolerable relations with his new hosts. During a German sweep he takes personal risk by saving a wounded guerrilla from capture. He even procures the first air drops of war equipment for the 34th ELAS regiment under Orestis – in spite of the British dislike of any uncontrolled armed force in the neuralgic zone near Athens.[4]

But after the outbreak of the inter-guerrilla civil war Stott cools off; in a signal to Cairo he denounces the alleged anti-British propaganda by EAM-ELAS and its "terror" against differently-minded Greeks.[5] At the same time Stott's old anger about ELAS' refusal to take part in the Asopos operation breaks through again.[6]

To some extent the captain is certainly influenced by his personal staff, consisting of some middle-class Greeks, fugitives from German captivity or otherwise connected with the resistance, but 'animated by anti-communist ideas'.[7] From the same circles Stott derives his "contacts" when he repeatedly enters Athens – for surgical treatment of a serious ear complaint (suffered at the blow-up of the Asopos bridge) as well as for sabotage work. For, in September Cairo resumes earlier projects aiming at the demolition of the main airfields and the aircraft located there in order to relieve pressure by the Luftwaffe on the endangered Aegean islands.[8]

Three reconnaissance trips convince Stott that there are no prospects for an immediate attack. Instead he decides to build up first an internal force in the periphery of the capital, then to infiltrate or to win over some able agents within the aerodrome staff.[9]

In Athens, hidden by the journalist G. Drosos,[10] Don Stott and his interpreter Kyrtatos pay a visit to P. Siphnaios, chief of the right-wing resistance organization Ethniki Drasis (National Action) which some weeks before took the lead in the foundation of PAS (Panhellenios Apeleftherotikos Syndesmos: Pan-Hellenic Liberation League), a loose alliance of about a dozen nationalist groups. After overcoming the initial mistrust, Siphnaios finally agrees on co-operation and arranges meetings with other right-wing leaders whether belonging to PAS or not. The young New Zealander manages to settle the existing personal jealousy between them as well as ideological aversions between royalists and republicans.

After a few days – presumably on 4 November – the representatives of eight organizations sign an agreement placing themselves under the orders of General Headquarters Middle East for carrying out sabotage and espionage, harassing the German withdrawal and preventing demolitions by them ("counter-scorch"). The signatories commit themselves to 'protect and help garrison' Athens during and following its evacuation by the Germans until the arrival of allied troops, thus preventing any possible *coup d'état*.[11]

The last clause undoubtedly hints at EAM, and Siphnaios promises to exert his influence upon King George II and the exiled Government to support this new course. For "Don" frankly confesses to his partners that he is acting on his own and that he has no sanction from his superiors, not to speak of an "order"[12] — as has been asserted subsequently.[13]

Stott's version is proved to be true by the reaction of SOE and of Woodhouse who also when informed of the first stage of those negotiations at once insisted: 'You should not, repeat not, take any part in political affairs. Your job is to sabotage enemy communication now and "counterscorch" on German withdrawal.[14] There exists at least one more message with the same meaning, so Stott — being aware of having infringed his competences — tries to keep back his story until his imminent return to the Middle East.

However, a critical report by the important Greek espoinage organization APOLLO compels "Don" to give his own account: 'Am not mixing in politics. Have great need for internal force in Athens to help sabotage operations. I have raised a united national non-political band of 12,000 officers and men eager to fight. Must see you personally on this subject.'[15]

There is no response by SOE, but even the Foreign Office — although permanently dreaming of a "counterweight" to EAM — reflects with considerable reservations on the recommended "non-political" union of groups of which 'many . . . are almost certainly genuinely patriotic', but others apparently have connections with collaborationist circles.[16] But even the majority of uncompromised organizations never received any real support from Cairo, since in the meantime their mentor and designated liaison officer — Don Stott — had compromised himself and within the same month leaves the Greek scene for ever.

Already in the middle of October Stott had been told by one of his rightist "contacts" that the German-appointed mayor Georgatos wanted to meet him, in order to prepare another meeting with a high German official. The latter would like to discuss "matters of mutual interest" and, according to a discreet hint by Georgatos, even a local peace proposal for Greece.

After an initial refusal "Don" reluctantly agrees, as on reflection (he) decided that no harm could come of such a meeting and that much useful intelligence might be gained.[17]

His still unknown antagonist is Colonel R. Loos, chief of the Secret Military Police in the Balkans. In the past Loos had repeatedly discussed with Georgatos the danger of Communism conquering all Europe as a consequence of the fatal German-British war. When Georgatos mentioned in confidence that his wife and some friends maintained relations with British agents, Loos asks for a meeting to be arranged. But knowing Hitler's suspicion of any "enemy contacts" he immediately informs the Plenipotentiary for South-East Europe, Neubacher, who manages by exaggerating . . . to obtain the *Führer's* half-hearted consent!.[18]

Simultaneously Stott signals to SOE that he had 'Met and had feelers put forward to me by a representative of Loos' — allegedly chief of the Gestapo — who 'has expressed an urgent wish to make proposals to be submitted to Cairo' with regard to Balkan problems.

The next day (8.11) SOE replies horrified and in an unusual hurry: 'You are required immediately in Cairo to report fully. Under *no* circumstances will any members of the Allied Military Mission have *any* contact or dealings with any Axis authority or officer or any person suspected of collaboration with the enemy. You will therefore immediately cease all negotiations with the Gestapo and return to Cairo...'[19]

But this veto does not reach Stott, as his wireless set fails to receive and soon also to transmit. Similar warnings by Archbishop Damaskinos, the chief of police Evert, and various leaders of the resistance are neglected by Stott[20], who informs Cairo on November 16 via APOLLO: 'Owing to lack of communication during the last six weeks I have had to make my own decisions. Germans expressed great wish to meet a British officer and finally contacted me. I have proposals to submit to British Government direct from Hitler. I have not committed myself, but am merely acting as courier.[21]

Three days before[22] one of the most curious "conferences" of the Second World War had taken place. Previously in some preliminary talks Stott had put forward four pre-conditions for his acceptance and Loos had agreed on every point: The meeting place — Georgatos' house — was given the status of neutral territory; a German officer (Karl Schürmann) was surrendered as a hostage to the Greek nationalists; Stott's safety was guaranteed and he was allowed to appear in British uniform (in order to assert the rights of a prisoner of war in case of German treachery.)[23] However, as an additional precautionary measure, the neighbourhood was to be guarded by Evert's armed men and by the Ethniki Drasis.[24]

Stott is accompanied by his two interpreters, Kyrtatos and Bakouros; the German side is represented by Loos, his interpreter Walther and the diplomat Rudi Stärker — the latter as representative of Neubacher, whose presence was forbidden by Hitler who wanted to confine the negotiations to a "medium level".

The atmosphere is tense until Bakouros' artificial beard coming unstuck produces the relief of laughter. Thereupon Loos and Stärker emphasize again the "irrationality of Anglo-German bloodshed" and therefore suggest negotiations on a separate peace the validity of which could be confined "for the time being" to Greece. Allegedly Hitler himself had approved of this proposal. This did not correspond to the facts. Hitler had merely allowed them "to throw out a feeler" and even this only since he was assured that it was the British who had taken the initiative, as the Germans on the spot wanted to put things in motion.

When Stott asks how the Germans would interpret the 'separate peace' if British landing troops entered Greece, he obtains the following assurance: A force of limited strength — just enough for 'keeping order' in Greece, but not capable of offensive operations northwards — would hardly meet with German resistance. 'In time there could be a smooth evacuation' in order to strengthen 'the German and European position' in Romania, already seriously endangered since the capture of Kiev and the encirclement of the Crimea by the Red Army.

Apparently the Germans admit that they are 'not yet' authorized by Berlin to commit themselves officially to this concrete pledge. But before carrying this matter further they would like an elucidation of British views.[25]

The proposed understanding is clearly directed against EAM-ELAS in the short-run and more especially against the further Soviet advance in Europe in the long run. Stott agrees to act "as courier" in this German attempt to split the Alliance, but it's not clear, whether throughout the discussion — lasting more than three hours — he had 'not committed' himself as he apologized to SOE. From the surviving participants Kyrtatos does 'not remember explicit anti-Communist manifestations' by Stott: Loos recollects only 'some hints' in this direction.[26]

In any case Stott consents to submit the German proposals. But first he wants to spy out the communications and defences round the Corinth Canal, as well as to take some files from his archives in Kyriaki. On the pretext of sending an advance signal to Cairo he persuades Loos to bring him to the Isthmus and from there by *caique** to the foot of Helicon. There Stott's German attendants wait in the *caique* until his return from Kyriaki the next day.[27]

On 19 (or 21) November Stott meets the Germans again. Although his wireless station on Helicon was out of order he gives fanciful details of his alleged communication with Headquarters in Cairo — which according to him 'took a great interest in the proposals' and wished to discuss them in the Middle East with German emissaries. At Stärker's request for an official invitation, Stott promises to do his best.[28] He gets the final German proposals into a metal tube and is allowed to take his assistants with him without any identification control. After the exchange of small parting gifts between Loos and Stott, the latter, his two interpreters and Siphnaios are brought by Schürmann in a big *Wehrmacht* car to Lavrion. There Schümann departs after having chartered a boat for the others who reach Chios on 24 November Thanks to Loos' recommendation the German commander of the island helps them in a friendly spirit and arranges their departure for Turkey.[29]

Meanwhile in Smyrna, Cairo and London the few initiated British officials are "anxiously waiting" for Stott's arrival and for an explana-

---

* *caique:* A sailing-boat (with or without motor) of the type used by fishermen and for transport in Greek waters.

tion. Immediately after the shock of the first "Gestapo" — message the FO had demanded from Cairo more details about Don's "serious misdemeanour". But even SOE does not know anything and suspects that the New Zealander had been trapped by the Germans and that he is not acting of his own will.[30]

In the meantime APOLLO had denied this suspicion, and therefore after their arrival in the Middle East Stott and his Greek companions were separated and throughout two weeks almost continuously cross-examined. In particular they were interrogated again and again as to how the contacts with the Germans came about and whether they had "compromised" themselves.[31]

At last the interrogators satisfy themselves about Stott's good faith, and on 21 December he even gets commended and decorated (with a bar to his DSO — awarded after the Asopos operation). In fact "Don's" last unorthodox adventure had provided not only concrete information on German installations in the Corinth Canal area — resulting in a successful British bomb attack, but also provided valuable intelligence about the enemy's internal situation. On the other hand, besides the suspension of his German contacts, even Don's pet idea of supporting his so-called "non-political" union is blocked for fear of renewing the Greek civil war.[32]

Nevertheless, a strong faction within Cairo SOE is still "anxious to send" Stott back to Greece for sabotage and "counter-scorch" operations already prepared by him in the autumn. But the SOE Headquarters in London with the byzantinist Talbot-Rice as spokesman vetoed this because of Stott's easy accessibility to foreign influences. Likewise the FO is afraid of new embarrassing tangles and so "Don" doesn't return to Greece.[33]

Now his traces begin to fade out. He is promoted to major and after home leave he is transferred for special service work behind the Japanese lines. On 20 March 1945 during a scouting trip to Borneo (Balikpapan) Stott's rubber dinghy fails to reach land. He and his three companions are reported missing, presumed killed. An adventurous life has come to a consistent end.[34]

This story, however, still needs more elucidation on the motives for Stott's activities. I take it for granted that for his negotiations no official permission, much less any order, ever existed. Apart from other quoted evidence Stott surely was not the type of agent who would have been entrusted with such a delicate task; SOE denies him 'any political judgement'.[35]

Such a deficiency can produce surprising results if combined with a personality like Stott's, of which a sharper outline should be attempted. In 1943 the New Zealander is a 29-years old athletic, courageous and self-convinced man, 'who always had to be doing something' as his compatriot Edmonds, senior Liaison Officer for Central Greece, properly summed up in his unpublished war memoirs.[36] His outstanding bravery repeatedly bordered on recklessness. So on one of his first days in Athens he startles his Greek attendants by his insistence on having a cup of tea in the fashionable "Zonar's", covering his uniform only with an old gabardine. Several similar incidents show him likewise prone to try his fortune.[37]

When he learns about the German "feelers" he is afraid of a trap, but at the same time his quick and daring mind grasps at the sudden chance to collect intelligence in a "smart" and sensational way and to distinguish himself by exclusive reports from the lion's (i.e. the Gestapo's) den. After his first contact with the Germans he becomes even more fascinated by reflecting on the possible developments. Therefore, after having returned to the safety of his old headquarters in Kyriaki, he does not go on to the guerrilla airstrip at Neraïda to take the usual route to the Middle East. First of all he wants to evade Woodhouse's rebukes for his "mixing in politics"[38], but mainly he is not contented with his partial success in Athens.

So he goes back there although even his sound nerves are rather strained now and in Cairo he will still be 'suffering from obsessions that he is being watched and followed by the Germans.'[39] Presumably that's why he gives them the cheerful news from his alleged communication with Middle East — he fears otherwise to risk his final return. But simultaneously he is full of expectation, as he tells his interpreter: 'I'll be the man of the day, if this succeeds!'[40]

Perhaps Stott is also influenced by motives similar to those of his German partners who are interested in taking even vague chances to promote an Anglo-German *rapprochement* and who therefore mislead Hitler as to the extent of British engagement[41], knowing the *Führer's* permanent fear of loosing face. But anyhow Hitler soon regrets his "concession". He gives orders to abandon the project without taking into account any British reaction.[42]

Meanwhile the British discuss Stott's escapades only with regard to their impending repercussions. The FO had immediately demanded 'all necessary steps . . . to prevent any risk of publication'. SOE urges APOLLO to use an additional security check in their signals in view of the 'present delicate situation'. And when Stott's 'soonest return' to Cairo is ordered, one of the main reasons given is that his 'contacts provide excellent propaganda material for certain Greek organizations.'[43]

But in spite of the calming assurances by the British censorship these "certain organizations" learn about the event with amazing speed — not by a German indiscretion as had been asserted but presumably from a camouflaged EAM sympathizer within the nationalist circles co-operating with Stott or Georgatos.[44]

Already on 28 November the EAM CC demonstrates its knowledge in a pertinent message to the exiled Greek cabinet and soon after to the three principal allied governments. Because of EAM's — justified[45] —

mistrust of the British-controlled communication system Moscow is additionally informed through two other channels: via Tzimas, the previous political adviser of ELAS, using the Yugoslav wireless system[46] and simultaneously by an EAM member within the American OSS (Office of Strategic Services) who informs the Greek "Anti-fascist Military Organization" in the Middle East ASO.[47]

On 17.1.1944 *Pravda* publishes a report by its Cairo correspondent referring to Anglo-German negotiations on a separate peace which had taken place in a European capital. A similar announcement follows by Radio Tiflis. When Churchill expresses telegraphically his consternation, Stalin re-assures him with a friendly but slightly ironical message.[48]

In fact the news from Athens undoubtedly increased Stalin's distrust of British secret policy and his permanent fear of some possible collusion with Germany. So perhaps Stott contributed unawares to the demonstrative Soviet renunciation of "intervention in Greek affairs" in order to restrain Churchill from any anti-Soviet adventures by leaving untouched his favourite playground — Greece.

However, Stott's activities had more tangible consequences for this country. Among them maybe the most important was the sincere belief of KKE and its related organizations that "Don" had acted with official British authorization. Thus in 1944 the political decisions of EAM[49] and of the ASO[50] were based on an understandable conviction that England was prepared to collaborate even with Fascist Germany against Communism.

But strange to say, Stott's talks and the British knowledge that EAM knew of them — prevented, until the end of the Occupation, an irreparable deterioration in their relations. For otherwise the BBC would probably have denounced ELAS for collaboration with the Germans[51] — based on a controversial event in Epirus which at any rate in no way resembled collaboration[52]

Moreover, the already-mentioned British decision to keep scrupulously aloof from Stott's anti-EAM union — in spite of secret sympathies and in spite of Tsouderos' urgent complaint to Churchill.[53] was itself of advantage to EAM.

Finally, another phenomenon, properly belonging to another scenario but somehow connected with the topic of this study should be mentioned.

When at the end of August 1944 the *Wehrmacht* started to evacuate the Greek islands by means of inadequate and improvised transport, the highly superior Royal Navy and Air Force contented themselves with a close but peaceful observation. Thus within twenty days the Germans managed to save most of their dispersed outposts. Both the High Command of the *Wehrmacht* and their Balkan staff presumed that this welcome indifference was due to conflicting Anglo-Russian interests in South-Eastern Europe.[54]

In fact the Soviets soon protested in London, Quebec and Dumbarton Oaks;[55] and simultaneously APOLLO warned SOE of this fatal passitivity[56] which created a "somewhat strange impression" even on these extreme Anglophiles.[57] Two days later (15.9) the RAF bombed the airfields near Athens and destroyed most of the German transport planes. But soon there was a new lull interrupted by frequent relatively ineffective attacks.[58]

So it's reasonable to conclude that Churchill connived at an orderly German withdrawal to the north as a pre-condition for building up a defensible Balkan front against the advancing Red Army. According to armament minister Speer's memoirs Hitler "unwillingly" agreed to a similar arrangement with London with a reciprocal promise to defend Salonica against a possible Russian assault till the British arrived on the spot. In a letter to me Speer insists on this version[59], in spite of British denials and although experience of British diplomacy as well as all German primary sources support the alternative of a *tacit* concurrence of interests.

In any case there exists a striking resemblance to the German offer of November 1943. Perhaps this is not unconnected with the remarkable post-war career of Rudi Stärker who left Germany rather quickly and entered the British Secret Services.[60] At the same time it's not too far-fetched to trace back his pertinacious taciturnity[61] to that very connection.

The fact that Stott's final report, the only one containing Loos's and Stärker's proposals, has not yet been released by the Foreign Office archives fits into the jigsaw. For, otherwise it might be seen that indeed some kind of British "answer" had been given ten months later: certainly no regular "local peace", but undoubtedly a temporary slow-down of war activities to a skirmish level, a slow-down due to a formal or – more likely – to a tacit understanding.

FOOTNOTES

1. Petros Rousos: I megali pentaetia 1940-1945. Vol.1. (Athens, 1976), p.509; similarly: Vasilis Nepheloudis: Ellines polemistes sti Mesi Anatoli. (Athens, 1945), pp.39f.; and many others.
2. Nikolaos A. Anagnostopoulos: I Evvoia ypo katochin. Vol.1 (Athens, 1950), pp.313, 316; Heinz Richter: Griechenland zwischen Revolution und Konterrevolution (1936-1946). (Frankfurt, 1973), pp.333, 348f.; Kostas Triantaphyllidis: in Apojevmatini 10/22.12.1964.
3. "Appointment of Lieutenant Donald John Stott, Second New Zealand Expeditionary Force, to be a Companion of the Distinguished Service Order – 1943. Official Citation" (Stott files, New Zealand; copy in my possession).
4. "Orestis", in: Akropolis, 7/8.6.61; Phoivos Grigoriadis: To antartiko. (Athens, 1964), Vol.IV, pp. 347f.
5. PRO (Public Record Office, London), FO 371/37206: R 10856; Pan. Siphnaios, letter 26.3.75.

6. The ELAS leadership was probably right in considering hardly feasible the SOE proposal of a full-scale attack against the heavily guarded Asopos viaduct. (Stefanos Sarafis: O ELAS, Athens, 1946, pp.98-9.)
7. Spyros Kotsis: Midas 614. (Athens, 1976), p.270. Among them was a son of the remarkable leader of the espionage organization BOUBOULINA, Lela Karayannis, who was executed by the SS in 1944.
8. Stott had been ordered to stage sabotage operations against the airfields of Kalamaki, Tatoi, Eleusis and Megara. ('Award of a Bar to the Distinguished Service Order to Captain Donald John Stott, D.S.O., Second New Zealand Expeditionary Force – 1943. Official Citation.' Stott Files, New Zealand; copy in my possession; herinafter cited as "Official Citation"). Other Sources: Arthur Edmonds, With Greek Guerrillas (unpublished memoirs 1942-44) p.107; Grigoriadis: *Op. Cit.*, IV, p.349.
9. Official Citation.
10. Drosos, however, stated to me that he had no knowledge of Stott's contacts and subsequent entanglement.
11. PRO. FO 371/43676: R 1046; NARS (US National Archives and Records Service, Washington), Rg 226: 130317; Christos Zalokostas: To chroniko tis sklavias. (Athens, n.d. = 1948), pp.231 f.; Siphnaios, letter. Representatives of the following groups took part in the conference: Ethniki Drasis RAN, EDES, EDEM, X, EKO, Triaina, and, remarkably, Major Seiradakis of the Intelligence Branch in the Rallis' Government's Ministry of Defence.
12. Zalokostas, *Op. Cit.* p.232; Siphnaios, letter 26.3.75; interview with Mich. Antonopoulos, Vas. Panagopoulos, Arch. Papadakos.
13. According to Richter (*Op. Cit.* p.347) Stott appealed to an ostensible "order to organize the Athenian Right". In this R. allegedly quoted Zalokostas, yet the latter reported just the opposite! *see* footnote 12.
14. "K" files (in private possession): signal NR 67, most immediate; the second part of Woodhouse's interesting signal continues: 'You should exclude EAM from cells organized by you but do it tactfully without letting them know you are doing so.'
15. AP (signals to and from APOLLO = Archives of Yannis Peltekis), APOLLO 159/14.11.43, 165/16.11.43.
16. PRO. FO 371/43676: R 1046. – This suspicion is justified at least as to Seiradakis, Grivas' "X" and the EDES faction represented by Colonel Papathanasopoulos.
17. Official Citation; interview with R. Loos.
18. Loos: interview and letter 27.12.72; Hermann Neubacher: Sonderauftrag Südost 1940-45. (Göttingen, 1956), p.203. Neubacher's version contains some mistakes, even concerning the year.
19. PRO. FO 371/37207: R 11604 – Loos' organization GFP (Geheime Feldpolizei) has ofen been confused with the Gestapo. Therefore in the Nuremberg trials the GFP was accused as a criminal organization but was acquitted.
20. Kotsis, *Op. Cit.* pp.272 f.; interview Antonopoulos/Panagopoulos/Papadakos.
21. PRO. FO 371/37208: R 12215; AP APOLLO 164/16.11.43.
22. Of the various dates mentioned by different sources the most probable is 13 November.
23. Official Citation; Loos, interview and letter 19.4.78. The preliminary meetings had been attended alternatively by Stott himself and/or his colleagues Morton and McIntyre.
24. Kotsis, *Op. Cit.* p.273; interview Antonopoulos/Panagopoulos/Papadakos.
25. Slightly differing: Loos: interview and various letters; interview Kyrtatos; Official Citation; Siphnaios, letter 26.3.75. Similiar proposals – to evacuate the Greek islands and preferably also the mainland at least up to Salonica

THE DON STOTT AFFAIR 101

– were repeatedly made by the German generals after the Italian capitulation but were always rejected by Hitler. (German records, *passim).*
On the contrary Kotsis *(Op. Cit.,* pp.269 ff. and interview) claimed that "most high German officers" were even ready to surrender to the British – a quite unreal version as not only the German officers were by no means inclined to such a radical break with their own "tradition" but neither did there exist any British forces able to "accept the surrender"!
This myth is largely due to a post-war report of Karl Schürmann, Loos' intimate. Schürmann born into a wealthy Athenian German family, successfully attempted, by that "modification" of the story, to appear as an anti-nazi and to secure his further stay in Greece which he was fond of. But though a proved philhellene he had likewise been an ardent admirer of Hitler, as confirmed even by his own sister (interview) with whom he had permanent ideological quarrels. Thus Schürmann's participation in an alleged conspiracy against the regime would have been "quite unthinkable".

26. Interviews Loos, Kyrtatos. According to Neubacher *(Op. Cit.* pp.203 f.) the New Zealander pleaded clearly for a joint drive against Communism, at the same time conceding that this 'is not yet the official opinion of the English government neither of the General Headquarters Middle East... but the view of a considerable portion of officers there'. Contrary to this, Loos supposed that N. – consciously or not – retained in his book the "amended" version once sent to Hitler, exaggerating Stott's anti-Communist engagement.
27. Loos: interview and letter 11.11.74.
28. Interview Loos; Official Citation.
29. Interviews Loos, Kyrtatos; Official Citation; P. Bakouros in Kotsis *Op. Cit.* p.275.
30. AP, Smyrna 116/19.11.43 and November, *passim;* PRO. FO 371/3702: R 11604.
31. Interview Kyrtatos; Siphnaios, letter 26.3.75. According to a sometimes unreliable source Stott had also to justify himself in a regular court-martial. (Pan. Rongakos, interview and letter 10.11.74; other authors: Kedros, Eudes etc. also base their accounts on Rongakos' statement.)
32. PRO. FO 371/43676: R1046; – /43684: R5591.
Stott allegedly managed to present his views to Churchill on the occasion of the 2. Cairo Conference (Zalokostas, *Op. Cit.* p.233; Rongakos, interview). In Greece he had referred repeatedly to his friendship with Churchill's son Randolph (Siphnaios letter), but this must not be overrated because then 'most British officers boasted of the same friendship' (interview Kyrtatos). However, if this story is true, Stott's talks with the premier remained without – immediate – results.
33. AP signals October/November 1943, *passim;* PRO. WO 201: 1598; FO 371/43674: R 225; –/43677: R 1718; –/43678: R 2015. Richter *(Op. Cit.* p.348) asserts – without presenting any evidence – that Stott returned to Greece and even draws conclusions from that allegation.
34. Stott Files; M.B. McGlynn: Special Service in Greece. (Wellington, 1953), p.31.
35. PRO. FO 371/37209: R 13356
36. Edmonds, *Op. Cit.* p.103.
37. Interviews Kyrtatos and Antonopoulos/Panagopoulos/Papadakos; Siphnaios, letter 26.3.75; William Jordan: Conquest without Victory. (London and Auckland, 1969), pp.132 f. Significantly Stott's SOE pseudonym was "Weasel".
38. G. Karayannis, in Kotsis *Op. Cit.* p.276; interview Kyrtatos.
39. PRO. FO 371/43674: R 225; interview Antonopoulos/Panagopoulos/

Papadakos.
40. Interview Kyrtatos.
41. An analogous game was played by Georgatos who largely exaggerated the position, influence and interest of Colonel Loos, in order to kindle Stott's curiosity. Thereupon the New Zealander reports to SOE that seven German generals had allegedly arrived in Athens especially to discuss "Balkan problems" with Loos, immediately after the latter's return from a — likewise fictitious — conference at Hitler's headquarters. (PRO. FO 371/ 37207: R 11604). By the way, six out of the seven named generals were imaginary too!
42. Interview Loos. Meanwhile Georgatos had let the news leak out in order to disturb relations between EAM and the British and to raise "prestige" and morale in collaborating circles. Now, at Hitler's command, Neubacher orders him 'to retract his statement as to the remote prospect of a separate peace with the English'. (NARS, Rg 226: 60338).
43. PRO. FO 371/37209: R 12215; — /37207: R 11604;
44. Loos: interview and letter 27.12.72; MA (Militär-Archiv Freiburg), 54961/ 1; LXVIII A.K. Ic, Report 11.3.44. NARS, Rg 226: 60338.
45. In 1943 (and still in 1944) Leeper had repeatedly intercepted, postponed or suppressed messages from and to EAM. (e.g.: PRO. FO 371/43686: R 7188; —/43690: R 11486).
46. PRO. FO 371/37209: R 12710; — /37210: R 13949; —/43686: R6579; Interview Tzimas.
47. Interview Vas. Nepheloudis; compare also: PRO. FO 371/43684: R 5066; NARS, Rg 226: 69246.
48. Correspondence between the Chairman of the Council of Ministers of the USSR, the Presidents of the USA and the Prime Ministers of Great Britain during the Great Patriotic War of 1941-1945. Ed. by the Ministry of Foreign Affairs of the USSR. (London, 1958), part I, pp.188 f., 191, 390 f.
49. MA, 65034/2, part 1 (NARS, Microfilm T 315, Roll 179, frames 869, 886): messages from GHQ ELAS and CC EAM to Tito (via Tempo) in January/April 1944, intercepted by the Germans. The same reason was given in discussions with many high-ranking members of KKE, EAM and ELAS.
50. Hagen Fleischer: The 'Anomalies' in the Greek Middle East Forces, 1941-1944, Journal of the Hellenic Diaspora, V: 3 (1978), pp.25f., 33.
51. C.M. Woodhouse: Apple of Discord. (London, 1948), p.168.
52. Grigoriadis *Op. Cit.* IV, pp.401 ff.; Dimitrios I Doumas: Istorikai anamniseis kai autoviographia. 2nd ed. (Ioannina, 1969), pp. 90 ff.; and many others. — This episode and generally all connections between the occupiers and the resistance will be dealt with fully in my forthcoming book on "Greece 1941-44". A brief survey has been given elsewhere. (H.F.: "Contacts between German Occupation Authorities and Major Greek Resistance Organizations: Sound tactics or Collaboration?" Paper delivered at the Symposium of the Modern Greek Studies Association, Nov. 1978; to be published).
53. E.I. Tsouderos: Ellinikes Anomalies sti Mesi Anatoli. (Athens, 1945), pp. 177 f.
54. NARS, Microfilm T 311, Roll 284; OB Südost Ic/AO, 7356/44 gKdos., 7422/44 gKdos. 16.9.44; Many other German sources.
55. Roland Hampe: Die Rettung Athens im Oktober 1944. (Wiesbaden, 1955), p.18.
56. AP, APOLLO 20/14.9.44.
57. Achil. A. Kyrou: Sklavomenoi Nikitai. (Athens, 1945), pp.185f.
58. MA 65721/2, 65721/3, War Diary "Heeresgruppe E" (Greece), Sept.-Oct. 1944, *passim;* and many others.

59. Albert Speer: Erinnerungen. (Frankfurt/Berlin, 1969), p.409; –, letter 8.12.75. – During the last occupation phase dozens of Anglo-German contacts took place, in the course of which the British usually demanded "unconditional surrender" but sometimes also hinted at a smooth-running "change of guard" – in one case even frankly referring to Don Stott. However, as in most cases Greek go-betweens of varying reliability were involved, the real significance of the negotiations is often disputable, Since I have compiled much pertinent unpublished material originating from all parties involved, I hope to deal with this topic in a separate study.
60. This is confirmed by three reliable and independent sources, two of them not mentioned in this report.
61. Having discovered Stärker's actual address with considerable difficulties, I asked him to express himself as to "some war events", and he agreed in principle. However, when he had ascertained which events I was interested in, he failed to answer my three (registered) letters!

DISCUSSION

Spyros Kotsis: (speaking in Greek from first-hand knowledge of the affair): I arrived in Greece in July 1942 with the Tsigantes mission from the Middle East – 12 people, though only 6 survived. I am in a position to have direct knowledge of the Don Stott affair since I was in charge of the mission for quite some time, after Tsigantes' murder.

After a telegram from Cairo I got in touch with Don Stott through his liaison contact, Kyrtatos, now a teacher of English at Athens College. Don Stott was responsible for the Attica-Boeotia area. Woodhouse, who was in charge after Myers left, assigned this area to him for carrying out sabotage.

Don Stott made three journeys to Athens and I met him at his third visit. He contacted the mayor of Athens Georgatos, who had been appointed by the Germans. Georgatos, wanting to be in an advantageous position after the war, which he saw that Germany was losing, proposed that he meet some Germans he knew, Welke and Loos.

Hagen Fleischer intervenes to deny the existence of Welke, probably confused with the non-commissioned interpreter, Walther.

Spyros Kotsis: Welke was a general and I don't know why he is hiding. He was directing all the discussions. These Germans wanted contact with a British officer to put forward proposals for defection from the Axis. They met at Georgatos' house. Loos, Welke, Kyrtatos, Schürmann, Bakouros, were all five present.

Hagen Fleischer (disagreeing): Schürmann was delivered temporarily as a hostage to Stott's companions McIntryre and Morton.

Spyros Kotsis: The majority of officers then in Greece were of Austrian or Hungarian origin. They knew Hitler was losing the war and wanted to defect. Loos and Welke said they knew another 15 high-ranking officers ready to collaborate and to hand over war criminals to be tried, in exchange for fair treatment for the German forces in Greece. They even offered themselves as hostages to accompany Don Stott to the Middle East if he did not believe them as they had understudies to carry out the project.

This was 13 November 1943. But Don Stott was acting on his own without Woodhouse knowing it.

Two days later he went to his Command post at Kyriaki on the Helicon by German *caique* to get some papers and documents and said to his agents there, many of them still alive to-day: 'You'll hear good news. But I can't tell you now. I'm going to Egypt'. But, when he left, they noticed he did not go towards the airfield but towards the Gulf of Corinth. (There was a secret allied airfield at Neraïda and one could be in Cairo in 2½ hours). But Don Stott could not use that service and did not go there because he was afraid of Woodhouse, since he was acting on his own initiative without instructions from the British. He also said he would go to London and come back again.

They met again on 21 November and came to an agreement. Welke and Loos gave him a boat. They went to Chios where they were caught but managed to find another boat, went to Asia Minor and then to Cairo.* The rest has been well presented by Dr. Fleischer — I suppose — as I don't know English *(Laughter in auditorium)*. Don Stott was decorated and sent to Burma. They did not want to send him back to Greece.

Hagen Fleischer: I believe that Mr. Kotsis' view — as presented in his book** — that in November 1943 the Germans offered defection *(apo-skirtisi)* and a surrender *(synthikologisi)* is absolutely unfounded and is completely out of the question, among other reasons because it is not in accordance with the spirit of the German *Wehrmacht.* There were no Hungarians in the officer corps, but there were Austrians. It was Loos who told me this story and that it came from Schürmann, a German whose family was established in Athens since 1890. When the Germans entered Athens, he joined the German Army and was a fanatical supporter of Hitler. But, on the other hand, he was a philhellene and, when he saw that the Third Reich was collapsing, he wanted to stay in Greece so he concocted a story, taking the fact of the separate peace offer and making it into something bigger in which he himself appeared as the main actor. In 1945 he told this story to Bouras, the Chief of Police and Mr Kotsis' superior, and so Schürmann got permission to stay on in Greece. This is where I disagree with Mr. Kotsis.

---

* Dr. Fleischer adds the following: "After the immediate breakdown of a boat supplied by the police and the MIDAS organisation (Evert, Kotsis, etc.) with Loos' consent, the Germans then placed a new and better boat at Stott's disposal. Naturally therefore, the little crew was not "caught" in Chios, but got a splendid reception from the local German garrison (Official citation; personal communication Loos and Kyrtatos)."

** Spyros Kotsis. 'Midas 614' *Athens,* 1976.

THE DON STOTT AFFAIR

Chairman: The point at issue is whether the object of the meeting between Stott and the German officers was as explained by Dr. Fleischer or whether there was some other German motive involving agreement on the withdrawal of certain officers and forces. I think it is just a matter of interpreting what the subject of the discussion was.

Spyros Kotsis: From the British point of view, what was the purpose of the peace offer by Loos and Welke?

Hagen Fleischer: Loos and Stärker aimed at the Soviet Union, in other words they wanted to end the Anglo-German confrontation and, if this was not feasible on a general scale, then at least locally. The Germans by way of suggestion offered to leave for Romania — a manoeuvre which would stop the Russian advance there, whereas the British could enter Greece as they wished.

E.H. Cookridge: Don Stott's story was obliquely told 22 years ago in Neubacher's book 'Sonderauftrag Südost'* which Dr Fleischer certainly knows, and was repeated many years later in 'Les Kapetanios' by D. Eudes.** I've researched in Coblenz and Freiburg, in the *Militärarchiv* and the *Bundesarchiv* for any reports from Athens. The only reference, a very vague one, was by SS Oberführer Stroop, chief of police in Athens. It was used by Dr. Julius Mahler and nothing but gossip emanated from the whole story. I must ask Dr. Fleischer to provide documentary evidence from German sources, as he says there are no sources from the Foreign Office or PRO. The Germans should have some reports in the *Militärarchiv* because there are lots of signals about negotiations with Mihailović. Moreover, Dr. Fleischer mentions Loos and Stärker which are German names and obviously belong to German officers, whereas the Greek speaker talks of Austrian and Hungarian officers.

Chairman: May I clarify the point? Are you questioning that the events actually took place or the evidence for them?

E.H. Cookridge: I don't know anything about whether the events took place or not. I know that Stott, when he was ill, was in the house of Archbishop Damaskinos in Athens. Whether he met any Germans or not I do not know.

Hagen Fleischer: As I said in the beginning, the evidence is from British, from Greek and partially from German archives.

E.H. Cookridge: Which British?

Hagen Fleischer: Foreign Office, Public Record Office.

E.H. Cookridge: Sorry. But you said before that there are no documents in the Public Record Office.

Hagen Fleischer: Only the final report, where at last you can see the motivation, has been removed.

---
* H. Neubacher. 'Sonderauftrag Südost 1940-45' (Special Mission South-East), *Göttingen*, 1956.
** Fayard, *Paris*, 1970; English Edition 'The Kapetanios'. New Left Books, London, 1972.

Chairman: Are there any German sources?

Hagen Fleischer: Neubacher did not send signals because he was a "flying emissary". Therefore the *Sicherheitsdienst* (Security Service) was not informed of the talks and German soldiers in Greece tried to keep the matter secret. There are only three short references to this affair. For example, in March 1944, it is mentioned that Voulpiotis is aware of the secret talks with Stott.

Bickham Sweet-Escott: I was in Cairo from the middle of December onwards as personal assistant to General Stawell who was the head of SOE Cairo. I didn't hear anything about any of this. Dr. Richter in his book* — of which I am ashamed to say that I have only just had the opportunity to read parts — mentions a limited enquiry in Cairo. I don't know anything about that.

Prof. Hammond: I would like to say that I tried to teach Don Stott Greek in Alexandria before he went to Greece and it was a hopeless task! He was a very delightful, brave and simple person. He went to Athens on his own initiative for an operation on his ear, so as not to be sent out of Greece.** According to the story, he stayed at a maternity hospital. I think it was on his own initiative that he decided to make contact with the German authorities, to try to negotiate a separate peace, like Dikaiopolis in a play of Aristophanes, the Acharnians.

E.H. Cookridge: Is it true that Stott was accompanied to Athens by ELAS men? A doctor gave him the name of a gynaecologist in Athens and that is how he came to be treated in the maternity hospital.

Markos Dragoumis (Press Councillor, Greek Embassy) Is it your view that he was under instructions and that he negotiated a separate peace or not?

Hagen Fleischer: I take it for certain that he had no order or permission and that he negotiated on his own. But I am not sure whether his initiative did not produce some consequences in 1944. Then, the pattern is nearly the same as what was proposed in 1943: not to harass, not to attack the Germans in their withdrawal to the north, in order to build up a stable defensive front against the common adversary, the Red Army.

Markos Dragoumis: And if were not for the Don Stott affair, this would not have happened, this tacit agreement?

Hagen Fleischer: That I cannot say because I don't have enough information.

Markos Dragoumis: I fail to see the relevance of this affair.

---

* Heinz Richter. 'Griechenland zwischen Revolution and Konterrevolution (1936-1946)'. Frankfurt, 1973.

** Dr. Fleischer adds the following comment: Professor Hammond is wrong here. Stott's famous operations for an abscess in the left ear was done in a maternity clinic in Athens on 17-18 July 1943 (SOE signals 291/177 and 318/19.7 to 'Mobility' *i.e.* the BMM main W/T station), that means more than three months prior to Stott's disputed contacts.

Hagen Fleischer: In Greek (and other) writings this affair has been quoted many times and, as I have said before, it is quoted as the reason for many decisive events, such as the founding of the Security Battalions and the outbreak of the internal guerrilla civil war. On the other hand, more seriously, the shocking and over-rated news of "Stott's mission" influenced the subsequent strategy of KKE, EAM and their kindred organisations in the Middle East, convincing their leaders that, in pursuit of their anti-Communist schemes, the British did not even desist from collaboration with Fascist Germany. That's why I thought it a good idea to get this affair into proportion, especially since I had had the chance to discover most of the surviving participants, as well as much relevant unpublished material, such as the APOLLO signals.

The Russian Mission to the Greek Mountains and entry of EAM into the Government of National Unity

Professor Nicholas Hammond

DISCUSSION

(paper not published at author's request, see Editor's Foreword)

George Catephores: "I heard with great interest your confident assessment that the role of the British Mission to Greece was purely military. Of course, in matters of diplomacy between the Resistance movements, the Greek Government and the British Mission, one cannot have a clear-cut view until all the archives are available; but I would like to raise a query about this purely military character of the British Military Mission. In C.M. Woodhouse's *Apple of Discord**, before the first serious clashes between EDES and ELAS, we find that Woodhouse was involved in encouraging Zervas to send a purely political message on the inflamed issue of the monarchy. I wonder whether you would describe this well-known message to the King as within the confines of a purely military mission.

Professor Hammond: I am not denying for a moment that politics are involved in military events. What I am saying is that the primary aim of the Mission was military. That was what we were concerned with and all officers were told not to get involved in the political aspects of the case, as happened with Don Stott. Of course, at the top level we were involved with matters which had political repercussions. For instance, we wanted to get the Resistance movements to act together and we were anxious that the King should say he would not return till there had been a plebiscite. That would, in the early days, have satisfied all three Resistance movements. To that extent we were involved in politics but what we were concerned with in Greece was primarily getting the people to go and fight the Germans. They understood the intention and did quite a lot but it went wrong. In the case of the EDES-ELAS-EKKA conflict this broke up the joint direction.

George Catephores: If you allow me to press this for a moment — the point at issue between Woodhouse and Zervas was not to suggest that the King would not return before a plebiscite but the opposite — Zervas was to send a message saying that he would support the return of the King whatever the attitude of the Greek people. This would not seem to contribute to a spirit of understanding among Greeks

---

* Hutchinson & Co. *London*, N.D. (1948)

but rather to inflame the mutual suspicion and possibly contribute to the clashes between the guerrillas. So one wonders whether the role of the British Mission was purely conciliatory or whether, by trying to apply this pro-royalist policy clearly indicated in early British decisions, it was not contributing to inflame the opposition between the Greek Resistance groups and, in this way, to the starting of the civil war.

Professor Hammond: I know nothing about this particular incident.

Brigadier Myers: There are two issues here: one is basically for the politician; the fundamental one is, was the Mission a military one? The short answer is "Yes". I was there at the beginning before we left Cairo for Greece, we were briefed solely about our military task, to obtain sufficient *andarte** support to cut the railway line to Piraeus. Woodhouse, my second-in-command, was to stay on with an interpreter and a wireless operator in case of further sabotage. It's as simple as that. We had absolutely no training. I was a soldier. I knew nothing about resistance movements – I learnt it all the hard way.

Now, on the second issue of Zervas' message, it happened in spring 1943, whilst I was away from H.Q. Aris Velouchiotis, the ELAS leader in Roumeli, had already given us considerable trouble. Our excellent speaker, Prof. Hammond, has talked of the "honeymoon period". But it wasn't real. We had trouble with ELAS from our first contact, but we managed to keep the ice from breaking. And because of the trouble with ELAS, Woodhouse went to Athens where he had met several members of the Central Committee and established for me and for Cairo and for London the character of EAM. It included one socialist party; otherwise none of the political parties had representatives on the Central Committee. They were all KKE (Communists) or trade unionists. Because of the trouble with ELAS, Woodhouse thought it would clear the air if Zervas were to send a signal to Cairo, saying in effect what we had been told – we had to stop people slanging the King of Greece; whenever anybody denounced the King we had to say it was contrary to our country's policy; he was our loyal friend who supported us, together with all your country's people when we were allies, and we had to remain loyal to him. To my mind it was not a question of Zervas being pro-royalist – opportunist, may be. He saved my life once and I owe him a great debt for that. Actually, he was loyal to me during my time in Greece and I believe, if while I was commander of the Mission we had asked him to stand on his head, he would willingly have stood on his head! And this was why he agreed with Woodhouse's suggestion that it would be helpful for the military effort – "All right. If you want the King back, I'll play to that tune" – Nothing more sinister than that. Of course, I realise that, knowing what happened afterwards, one can read into it things a lot more sinister than that. By then I myself had already told Cairo at

---

* The Greek word for guerrilla, *lit.* rebel.

least once about the importance of a plebiscite about the King before he came back. This would have taken away one of the main planks from ELAS' platform and would have increased the chance of getting a greater military contribution from the *andartes*.

Chairman: I wonder whether making Zervas stand on his head would be considered a military or a political act?

Contribution from the auditorium: I find it very difficult to believe that the British liaison officers in Greece were playing the role of benevolent referee between the warring Greek sides, whilst the Soviet delegation had other things in mind. I believe we've seen that British liaison officers did play a political role. Brigadier Myers mentions in his book 'Greek Entanglement'* that, by January 1943, the web of Greek politics was surrounding us and, at least from then on, they played a political role. One does not have to read Clausewitz or Engels to understand that military policy is the extension of politics. I would also add that I heard Prof. Hammond call Siantos an agent.

Prof. Hammond: A Russian-trained agent. At the time of Metaxas, these people were in Moscow and they came back — I would say — as Russian-trained agents of communist persuasion.

The previous contributor: Siantos admitted he had been trained in Moscow but, from his youth, he had participated in the tobacco-workers' struggles.

Professor Hammond: I am not denying that. These were deeply convinced and very genuine communists. I am not criticising them for that at all. What I was explaining was the extent to which Russia influenced the Resistance movements in Greece. It influenced them in this way: it trained people who were in fact leaders, political leaders like Siantos, Tito, Hoxha — they came back trained not only in communist organisation but also for resistance movements. It is undeniable that all these movements had the same structure. Then they sent the three Russian colonels who, as I said, had nothing to offer, so that Russia's last effort was a damp squib...

Chairman: I think the first question raised was the relationship between political and military aims. Would you like to answer that question?

Prof. Hammond: Your term "referee" is a correct one. That is exactly what we were. We were trying to keep Greeks united in fighting the Germans. I think all will agree that was a sensible aim in time of war. We supplied ELAS as much as anyone else, except when they fought other people.

Contribution from the auditorium: This is not exactly a question, it is something, I hope in support of Prof. Hammond. I was one of the liaison officers and certainly we had instructions to be a *military* mission. We had to keep the different partisan groups together to fight, but it wasn't easy. We were constantly drawn into the web of Greek

---

* Hart-Davis. *London*, 1955

politics. To give you an example, I had conversations with a right-wing group on one occasion. I went on to say exactly the same things to a left-wing group and I was accused by the latter of going round telling everybody that the British were favouring the right. Now, that was the last thing I was saying. I was trying to be as useful as I could, but what happened was that the right-wing Greeks were telling their friends "the British are on our side and are giving us the arms" and, at that stage, the left-wing Greeks believed it. And sometimes *vice versa*. It was extremely difficult; although our instructions were to fight a military battle and not get involved in politics, it was difficult not to be involved in politics.

Christos Alexiou: I heard Prof. Hammond say that he met many communists and some important ones. In his preface to Kousoulas' book* Woodhouse writes that the Greek communists are everything the Greek people are not: the Greek people are patriotic, the Greek communists are not; the Greek people have *filotimo*** the Greek communists have not — and so on and so forth. With such a hatred for communists, could Woodhouse be objective?

Professor Hammond: I can't speak for Woodhouse. I can say that I met many communists and made friends among them. I knew Siantos, we talked freely on many subjects and I admired him in many ways but I didn't admire the methods ELAS used on his instructions — that's a different issue. As regards the qualities of the communists, I would say they have the same qualities as any other Greek.

Question from the auditorium on the contribution of ELAS to the struggle against the Germans.

Prof. Hammond Of course, without ELAS we would never have been able to mount the operations against the various railway lines and to do what we did to destroy German units. ELAS carried out successful operations on its own and they also gave us a platform to carry out operations. The Greek Resistance movements, all three of them, did a great deal, ELAS perhaps in some ways more, to keep up the morale of the Greek people and to discomfort German units. I would have liked to see that all the time. But we got those splits developing.

The previous questioner: I asked you what was your attitude towards ELAS at the time?

Prof. Hammond: I was liaison officer with ELAS and my job was to get them to attack the Germans and not other people and I had supplied them with a lot of material. In Macedonia, for instance we had large sums of money coming in. In the three months I was there we

---

* 'Revolution and Defeat: The story of the Greek Communist Party' by D. George Kousoulas, O.U.P., 1965.
** A practically untranslateable word, perhaps best rendered by "sense of honour" or "personal pride".

raised the strength of the units up to 3,000 men by supplying equipment.
The questioner: That was your job. You as a person what was your attitude?
Prof. Hammond: One of friendship. You can't have a personal attitude towards a movement. I was not politically interested in ELAS but in whether they would fight.
Andreas Kedros: Prof. Hammond said that many times he had to cut off supplies from ELAS because the British did not want to supply ELAS so that it could fight Greeks. I would like to ask if he remembers whether supplies to EDES were cut off? And whether the Military Mission was able to establish responsibility for the clashes?
Prof Hammond: The point was that I told you this in detail so that you could see how things work on the ground. The *British liaison officer* at the scene of action sees what is happening, say with ELAS and EKKA. He sends a message to H.Q. saying "Look, ELAS troops are fighting against a certain group" for example, against EKKA. It was the responsibility of *the man on the spot* to report to H.Q. who had started it. We had no better evidence than that. It's the evidence which directed us, as representatives of the Western allies. We stopped supplies to that movement which, in our opinion, started a civil war. We didn't stop supplies to the people who were attacked. I think that's logical.
Contribution from the auditorium: We heard something this morning about the popularity of the Resistance movements and of reports sent back by some diplomats that they were extremely unpopular and that the population came to fear them more than the Germans.
Prof. Hammond: The first year the peasants were all in support and one was absolutely safe moving amongst peasants in Thessaly. I thought it quite safe to go to Salonica, as I did not expect to be betrayed by any Greeks if they found out our linkage. There were, of course, some who would but I did not expect the people generally to be against us or against EAM-ELAS at that time. In the later stages, when the five months of civil war had caused great loss of life and terrible distress to the peasant population of the whole area of W. Pindus and into Epirus and some of the areas of Thessaly and Macedonia — I was in a village where the ELAS HQ was and there were executions every morning, mainly civilians — there was a great fear of all the Resistance movements towards the end. But there was always support for the Resistance movement in the cities because of the image of the Resistance — and rightly. You see, resistance movements are only conducted by people who are very extreme in their attitudes to life. If you are a pacifist or a person who dislikes reprisals, then you don't take part in resistance. You have to read Anouilh's 'Antigone' to understand this.
Contribution from the auditorium: A few minutes ago you, yourself distinguished between what you did not question: the sincerity of the movement, and its actual function in an historical situation, I wonder

whether you could apply this distinction of yours and ignore for the moment whether anybody's sincerity or belief is on trial and answer the question as to what objective historical results followed from the so-called military presence, in particular in what way did it lay the foundation for Churchill's programme of confronting by force the legitimate aspirations of the Greek people? *(Applause)*

Prof. Hammond: I am not talking about Churchill. I am talking about the military mission, its aims and what it achieved and, in particular, its relation to the Soviet Mission and PEEA, the entry of EAM representatives into the Papandreou government. As I ended up, it brought the Greek Resistance movements together, to fight the Germans as they withdrew. Both Sarafis and Zervas placed their forces under the command of General Scobie when his troops came in, and all operated together with the Raiding Support Regiments* we brought in and that was the primary military aim. The second aim, as I said all along, was to try and keep the resistance forces from fighting each other, rather getting them together and, in the last stage, into the Government of National Unity which gave a chance of a peaceful solution, if only the Greeks would agree amongst themselves. That is as far as I am going. I don't want to get into discussion of December 1944. I wasn't there and I know nothing about it.

Brigadier Myers: If the British Mission had not gone to Greece, ELAS might well have overcome all opposition in the mountains. EDES might have been virtually obliterated and EKKA would not even have stood a chance to exist. If the British Mission had not gone to Greece therefore, the British Government, and especially Churchill, would have been in a much less strong position to support the Greek King in exile.
(Uproar in auditorium)

George Petrochilos: Even with the benefit of hindsight, I am amazed to hear that, if the Military Mission had not gone there, EAM-ELAS would have had it all their own way. The answer is: so what? What was wrong with it? Why did we need more resistance groups? Was it because some of them were to be used for the nice British political game of "divide and rule?"

Chairman: I think the answer to your question is really related to the previous one as to whether the objective of the Mission was military or political.

George Yanoulopoulos: Professor Hammond, you said that the British were not exactly pleased with ELAS because they were not fighting the Germans all the time. Now, assuming that there is some continuity in British policy which transcends individuals and we can look at it over the years, how can we explain the contradiction, that, on the one

---

* Special British units trained to enter occupied countries, and operate alongside guerrillas against the Germans.

hand they were not pleased with ELAS because they were not fighting the Germans all the time and, on the other, at later stages they did support Greeks who have not been accused of fighting against the Germans and even Greeks who have been accused of fighting with the Germans?

Prof. Hammond During the period of which I was talking, we were pleased with ELAS when they were fighting the Germans.

George Yanoulopoulos: No I am talking about later stages.

Prof. Hammond: We were not pleased when they were fighting other Greeks and started that fighting. This is, I think quite clear. With regard to those who fought on the German side, we had them publicly condemned in broadcasts. There was no question of collaborating with the Rallis forces and the Security Battalions.

George Yanoulopoulos: I am not saying that you did it at that time but, assuming that there is some continiuty in British policy and we can judge its consistency on this basis. . .

Prof. Hammond: When you win a war you move into an entirely different phase of politics. I quite agree but I'm talking about this wartime period only and, as I see it, the Mission had a primarily military purpose and it carried out that purpose, I think effectively. The trouble within, this was a thing that went back to 1936. There were a great many strains and tensions in Greece due to political events. First of all, the collapse of the Venizelist type of democracy: the ins and outs, one-day dictators and finally a government which turned into Metaxas; then the point that Metaxas, despite the fact that everybody disliked him and the British as much as any because he was of the fascist type, nevertheless brought Greece into the war and so on — all these strains which came out in the different resistance movements. But it was not our concern to sort out your differences, what we wanted to do was to get these movements to combine against the Germans and in the end, if we could, get them all into one government and let them try to work out their own future.

Christos Alexiou: Professor Hammond, you said that in 1943 you tried to bring the resistance movements together in Macedonia: Vasilis Samariniotis and PAO. You said that ELAS was intransigent. You didn't mention why they were intransigent. ELAS, even EDES and EKKA, cannot well be put on the same basis as PAO. As far as I know, PAO was not a straightforward Resistance movement. There were many collaborators in PAO, very notorious people, and the ELAS leaders had good reason not to accept collaboration with PAO.

Prof. Hammond: You may be right but the point is that the EAM representative in Salonica signed an agreement with them whilst I was there, that is with the representative of YVE and the EDES people in Salonica participating, and the agreement was conditional upon EAM approving it. Then that report went to the joint HQ of which the heads of ELAS were members and they approved the admission of

THE RUSSIAN MISSION TO THE GREEK MOUNTAINS 115

PAO. What Kikitsas and Markos were doing was not implementing that decision and that was contrary to the approved policy of HQ. Middle East and of ELAS.
Yanis Yanoulopoulos: You mentioned in your talk that there were conditions, what were they?
Prof. Hammond: I think to get rid of certain people.
(Laughter in auditorium)
Prof. Hammond: That was true of all movements. There was always the danger of double-agents getting into the movement. ELAS got rid of people...
Contribution from the auditorium: There were German collaborators in PAO.
Prof. Hammond: Not the ones I was with, because they would have betrayed me to the Germans when I was in Salonica. I was with three colonels, Mousterakis, Argyropoulos and one other. Argyropoulos went out to Egypt and fought with the troops there. You see, the Greek forces outside Greece were also fighting the Germans.
E.H. Cookridge: Many good friends have asked questions about the attitude of members of the Mission. They seemed to think the Mission had only one attitude. Perhaps Prof. Hammond will say a few final words about the Sheppard report.
Prof. Hammond: Sheppard and I were the first two liaison officers with ELAS and he reported very favourably about them. He did not speak Greek, he had an Egyptian Greek as an interpreter and he believed everthing Karayiorgis told him. On the other hand, I took three Greeks in with me: one a young officer, another a left-wing Royal Airforce engineer, and a wireless operator who had no particular interest in politics. The unit I was with was a unit of 15 men. We were together for 6 weeks on Mount Ossa (Kissavos) in the snow and we got to know each other extremely well. Naturally, with my knowledge of Greek, I got to understand the movement's thought more deeply than Sheppard did and his report was much more favourable to ELAS than mine was.
Prokopis Papastratis: There is a directive of the Foreign Office to the BBC in June 1944 which said "Stop direct attacks on the Security Battalions".
Prof. Hammond: I do not know this at all.
Prokopis Papastratis: I don't remember the date but I can give you a photo-copy*.
Thanasis Hajis: Did the Military Mission know that the founder and leader of PAO was Chrysochoöu who was apparently appointed by the collaborationist government as Inspector of the Prefectures of Northern Greece? After the incident at the Haliacmon river where PAO forces collaborating with German troops prevented a joint operation by ELAS

---

* Greek Directive dated 22 June 1944, FO to Cairo. Repeated to Washington on Tel. 5643, R8041, FO 371/43706

and British officers to blow up the bridge, did not the British Military Mission receive a telegram from HQME condemning PAO as a traitor organisation in the sevice of the Occupation? When the Joint Guerrilla GHQ was formed and there was discussion of a proposal by the then Head of the BMM for the acceptance of PAO as an equal member, was not the proposal rejected because of the revelations about its treasonable activity? And, at the same meeting, was not a proposal by Zervas that PAO be regarded as forming part of his organisation in Macedonia also rejected? Therefore PAO was not a national resistance organisation but a traitor organisation in the service of the Occupation and as such was fought by EAM-ELAS and condemned by HQME. There is a relevant passage in Field-Marshal Sir Henry Maitland Wilson's book 'Eight Years Overseas'.*

The above incontrovertible facts did not prevent the British from making contact with these traitors and even with Chrysochoŏu himself, sending Major Eggs** of the BMM to Salonica for this purpose.

Prof. Hammond: I'm afraid I don't remember who the founder was. I have no doubt that Mr. Hajis is correct; but the question was, was PAO worthy and did it come out and fight at that time, mid-summer 1943? It was judged so by Joint HQ. The appearance of PAO near Elafina did upset the plans we had to blow up the Haliacmon bridge and we were extremely annoyed that it did so. It drew the Germans' attention to the fact that there were considerable allied forces in lower Pieria and this meant we could not go ahead because the Germans were alerted. As to PAO being approved by the Joint HQ it certainly was approved and they sent Mousterakis to take the message to Salonica but he was intercepted on the way and imprisoned.

In conclusion, George Catephores, as translator for Mr. Hajis, re-affirmed that the latter maintained there had been no such decision.

PANEL DISCUSSION

The Chairman (Prof. R. Doganis) introduces the panel:
George Catephores (Lecturer in Economics, University College, London)
Richard Clogg (Lecturer in Greek History, King's College, London)
Brigadier E.C.W. Myers (Head of the wartime British Military Mission to Greece 1942-43)
Bickham Sweet-Escott (wartime senior SOE operative)

Questions from the auditorium: When did the British officers who came

---

* Hutchinson and Co., *London*, N.D. 1949
** *Nom-de-guerre* of Professor Hammond

to Greece become SOE operatives? and how many British liaison officers were there?

Brigadier Myers: They were operating under SOE from the very beginning. Our agent in Athens, under the pseudonym "Prometheus", sent a message saying that, if some sabotage officers could be sent in by a certain date or between certain dates, then it would be possible to cut the railway line to Piraeus. This was sent to SOE Cairo and thus it was from the very beginning. On the second point, when I left Greece in the summer of 1943 there were already between 30 and 40. Our idea was to have a British liaison officer, subsequently reinforced by American liaison officers, with every ELAS band and with every band of any other organisation that was worth noticing. So, as Prof. Hammond has already indicated, we were in touch with the picture and with the problems resulting from any attack on them or attack by ELAS on other bands which, unfortunately, happened only too frequently.

Professor Hammond: By the end there were, I think, about 80 north of the Isthmus of Corinth and perhaps 30-40 in the Peloponnese, and there was another group in Crete. The two first were under my general command but, in fact, one had little to do with the Peloponnese. The main centre of the British Mission was in northern Greece.

The previous questioner: Were there any American officers?

Professor Hammond: Oh yes! By the end the Americans were with us all along the line.

Bickham Sweet-Escott: I think it is fair to add that there were no British liaison officers in the Ionian Islands at that time, late 1944.

Chris Carratt: There were also 1,000 Americans of Greek origin broken up into companies of 100 and dispersed around the country. I'd like to point out to Professor Hammond, who questions the popularity of the Greek resistance movements, that towards the end I was under the impression that we were becoming terribly unpopular and, if we had gone through a third winter, it would have been a completely different story. The numbers of the Security Battalions were growing and there were certain villages where we could not operate. I personally was stoned by Greek women in villages near Elassona when I was with the ELAS guerrillas because we wouldn't stand and defend the villages and it was only when "Noah's Ark"* came along towards the end that we could really operate in those areas again. But we were becoming very unpopular.

Prof. Hammond: I would agree. Towards the end you did not feel safe in areas which were not immediately under the control of EAM-ELAS because of the opposition to it. It may have been the same in EDES areas — I don't know. The point was that the cost of the resistance

---

* Code-name for the allied landing operation in Greece at liberation in September-October 1944.

movement was mounting all the time. The number of burnt villages was very, very large and, you see, when an operation was carried out, the Germans conducted reprisals by killing large numbers of hostages. If you killed 30 Germans by derailing a train, they might kill 100 Greeks. The question was, was it worth it? And of course it built up opposition amongst the people who were in danger of being shot. This was an inevitable feature of the resistance movement.

Bickham Sweet-Escott: I might add to that, Mr. Chairman, that I almost got court-matialled for suggesting that "Ill met by moonlight" should be cancelled because it was to take place in March 1944, when everybody knew that the war was coming to an end so far as Greece was concerned instead of three years before. And they got the wrong general anyway. He was quite unpopular but not as unpopular as his predecessor whom they were after. And the result was that 208 Cretans were put against the wall and shot*.

Brigadier Myers: Mr Chairman, I think it's opportune if I make a couple of general remarks now — it'll take me two to three minutes.

When we went to Greece, we had not won the war, we were not even winning the war, the tide was just turning but we didn't know that at the time. We were sent to Greece with a specific mission, to help Montgomery in his breakout at El Alamein by cutting one of the two main routes for supplies to Rommel. Of course, by the time we'd finished, the outcome of the war was in no doubt. When a war is in doubt, resistance movements are a jolly good asset — the more bangs the better and then there is the morale-raising factor of having the *andartes*** moving about the mountains of Free Greece. But this also had a wider effect — it was internationally morale-raising. I do not wish to appear vain about our achievements, but the success at Gorgopotamos*** raised people's tails far beyond the boundaries of Greece. On the other hand, though Operation "Animals" in conjunction with the invasion of Sicily† was successful and contributed in a major way towards the success of the invasion, it was probably relatively less important from the morale point of view.

The second point is that, whereas in Yugoslavia the mountain areas are extensive and lend themselves to wide-spread overt resistance against the enemy, the mountain areas of Greece are comparatively

---

* This refers to the kidnapping of the German General Kreipe by two British liaison officers in Crete, described in the book 'Ill Met By Moonlight' by W Stanley Moss, Harrap & Co., *London*, 1950.

** the Greek word for guerrillas, *lit.* rebels.

*** the blowing-up of the bridge over this river on the main north-south railway line by a force of ELAS and EDES guerrillas with British saboteurs under the command of the speaker on 25 November 1942.

† A series of operations all over mainland Greece in summer 1943 calculated to deceive the Germans into expecting an allied invasion there instead of in Sicily.

small and not so suitable for carrying out resistance, and it always used to make me feel very afraid every time I heard of a major German sweep coming up the mountains to see us off. The point is, they never managed it. Thanks to the successful operations elsewhere, they never had the time and the men available to do it properly — anyhow in my day. But I think you cannot take these things in isolation and, coming back to the beginning, we did achieve a military object.

George Catephores: I'd like to try to clear up this question of PAO as far as possible. You, Professor Hammond, mentioned in response to a question some reservations about PAO — that it should rid itself of some suspicious elements. Was that in the Joint GHQ decision?

Professor Hammond: Yes, in the decision of the Joint GHQ.

George Catephores: So would you say that the disagreement between you and Thanasis Hajis is based on a different interpretation of that decision: you saying that they got the green light subject to this purge and Thanasis Hajis saying that, to get the green light, they would first have to get rid of these elements and then apply again to Joint GHQ on the basis that they were now a dependable force, so that in that case there would be a different decision?

Professor Hammond: What had in fact happened was that the Joint GHQ recommendation never reached PAO because, as I said, EAM-ELAS did not pass it through to them. The PAO people having been encouraged to come out because of this agreement even though it was still not entirely unconditional because EAM had to approve it, nevertheless came out because they thought we wanted to get started. What I objected to was Kikitsas and Markos preventing them from getting a foothold despite the recommendation from Joint GHQ.

Thanasis Skouras: It would seem that military objectives were pursued within a clear and well-defined framework of political objectives. Following the doubts expressed by George Catephores about the Command's exclusive concern for greater military efficiency, it seems to me that it should have been quite easy to achieve this if you had ordered Zervas — who was prepared to stand on his head* — to join in with ELAS; you wouldn't have to disband his force, you just had to subjugate it to the unified command which would obviously be dominated by ELAS. Clearly, the fact that you didn't act quite like that indicates that the political objectives had already been set and it was within this framework that military objectives were pursued.

Professor Hammond: What you are really suggesting is that the alternative for the British Mission was to put all its support behind EAM-ELAS and build it up so that it would dominate the whole of Greece. That would undoubtedly have resulted in Greece, Albania and Yugoslavia all being communist-controlled under the three communist move-

---

* see page 109

ments. I'm telling you what the result would have been...
Interruption: But this is involvement in politics! (*Uproar*).
Professor Hammond: We thought — and I think rightly — that if you want resistance in Greece, you want it from all sections of the population, not just from the communists.
Thanasis Skouras: But if it was only efficiency you were concerned with, that consideration would not have carried any weight.
Professor Hammond: I don't think ELAS was the most efficient of the three military units.
at this point Mr Sweet-Escott apologised for having to leave early and thanked the organisers of what he described as a fascinating seminar.
Chairman: Can we have a comment from Brigadier Myers?
Brigadier Myers: I wish it was as simple as that. As I already said, initially we had no political directive whatsoever. We, and SOE Cairo, were the first people to draw attention to the growing political problem inside Greece. We went in in September 1942; in the very early days — let's start in February — I was getting a fairly clear idea what EAM-ELAS stood for, what their aims were and what the problem was between EDES and them. And, as some of you who have read my book will know, I was sending back fairly long signals to HQ in Cairo about this situation which was becoming rather complicated. At the same time Cairo was getting reports from Colonel Sheppard on Mount Olympus about how wonderful ELAS was (this was shortly before Nicholas Hammond arrived) and they were confused and inclined to believe what Sheppard was telling them and saying couldn't I be mistaken by getting too much propaganda from Zervas? Well, by that time Woodhouse had been to Athens where he met the EAM Central Committee and we had become even more reinforced in our ideas. The political thing wasn't so clear to the British for a long time, although the FO knew something about EAM from the early days and SOE a little about EAM-ELAS. When we were sent into Greece, we had no briefing about EAM-ELAS at all, we were not told of their existence, we were going to drop on a band belonging to a chap called Seferiadis who belonged to no political organisation at all, as far as I can remember, certainly not to EDES. On the other hand, Woodhouse was supposed to drop to EDES and, as I told you before, it was weeks before we got in touch with any ELAS bands. We had to find them, not they us, and these were Aris' bands in western Roumeli who came over to help. The FO only very gradually developed a policy for our dealings with these problems in the mountains and it was not a black-and-white policy. Gradually a British political policy for Greece became known to us, superimposed on the paramount aim of winning the war and this is why I eventually got unseated because the two became so interwoven and the only chance to gain the maximum military effort — as I saw it — was by acquiescing in the demands which were general throughout all republican bands about political objectives at the end of the war.

PANEL DISCUSSION   121

Markos Dragoumis (Press Councillor, Greek Embassy): I'd like to ask Professor Hammond one question and Brigadier Myers another question. The first question is what, in your view, was the perception of the British Mission in Greece regarding the differences between the feuding resistance movements? I'm not asking what they thought of each other but what was your assessment of their differences? The second question is: what was, again in your view, the reason why EAM-ELAS was so much stronger than the others?

Professor Hammond: On the first question, EAM-ELAS thought, I think, that they ought to have complete control of Greece and they resented the presence of any other movement. Wherever I went in Macedonia or Thessaly, I heard people making speeches against EDES, denouncing them as traitors. Whether they really believed they were traitors I don't know. If I had been in the EDES area, I would probably have heard people saying that ELAS were traitors. It was the same between ELAS and EKKA. We were not getting involved in these arguments. What we were saying was: "If you'll fight against the Germans, we'll give you supplies (and we did so) but if you're going to fight each other, we won't give you supplies." If you ask how efficient ELAS was; well, ELAS spent 5 months fighting EDES. This was not, from our point of view, efficient at all.

To the second question, I'll explain this on the grounds that KKE were the first to go into the field and they were more capable organisers. They were republicans and there was a lot of feeling against Metaxas and the King. They had a very good programme and they made a very simple demand; that everyone joining them would take an oath to stay with them until a plebiscite was held to determine whether the King should return. They had a very wide appeal in Greece. In the first unit I was with there was only one person I would say I knew that he was a communist, none of the others were. The number of communists was very small but they had an extremely effective and efficient organisation from the point of view of bringing in recruits and it did a very good job.

Brigadier Myers: I'll just add a few words to that which will reinforce what Nick Hammond has said. Ever since Metaxas came to power, KKE members had either been arrested or had gone underground and the result of the 6 years of Metaxas' rule and the short period that followed (1936-42) was that KKE had become experts at establishing underground cells and these existed in all the small towns and even in some of the larger villages all over Greece. And the moment EAM started, these people started forming cells all over Greece — with one or two exceptions — and of course the obvious exception was Valtos from the time Zervas went there. He went there because it was his home area where he had been brought up and he knew it. His area of operation was confined to that. His was never a widespread nation-based organisation; whereas EAM-ELAS was geographically widespread from the start, spreading out from the urban areas and from quite small ones too.

Richard Clogg: I'd like to go back to the point made by George Catephores and Thanasis Skouras about whether or not the British either encouraged the unified Greek resistance or tolerated ELAS' efforts to dominate the resistance in the interests of military efficiency. Brigadier Myers has written* – and I think this is generally accepted – that, when his Mission went into Greece in the the autumn of 1942, ELAS (for whatever reason) was not anxious to participate in any major operations. They may have had good reasons but they were not anxious. On the other hand, Zervas was ready and willing. In the aftermath of Gorgopotamos,** when Zervas knew that ELAS had been dragging its feet, it would have been ludicrous to expect him to submit to ELAS' command on the grounds of greater military efficiency. He would have said "this is totally absurd" and he would have been quite right to say so.

Prokopis Papastratis: I'd like to make two points. On the issue of the Security Battalions, I'd like to point out that in early May 1944 their inclusion in the post-war National Army was under consideration in the Middle East. At the same time the FO directive to the BBC to stop attacking the Security Battalions was issued. On supplies to the Greek resistance movements, I'd like to point out that, between the end of the Lebanon Conference and the end of June 1944, Zervas received 132 tons, ELAS 31 tons and the other *capetans*† 6½ tons. And, of course, the war was going on and 'Noah's Ark' was in preparation. I'd like to ask George Alexander to elaborate on the following point. In his paper on events in the Middle East, he completely disregards the decisive British intervention on the side of the Greek government-in-exile. Their intervention comes out so clearly from the documents in the Public Record Office that we cannot ignore it. But George said that he deliberately left the British out of account.

George Alexander: I left it out deliberately because I don't think the story suffered by this being left out. Papandreou was selected by the King to be the new premier and the British gave him their support – reluctantly at first at least as far as the Southern Department was concerned – mainly because Churchill backed the King's judgment. The British gave support to Papandreou because, at that time, they wanted somebody as prime minister of the government-in-exile who would be able to pull all the parties together in a united government. The last thing they wanted was for Greece to be politically split. So I explained the policy of Papandreou and don't see why I should include the British who supported his policy.

---

* in his book 'Greek Entanglement'. Hart-Davis, London, 1955. pp. 72 and 275.
** For Gorgopotamos see footnote to p.118.
† guerrilla leaders, *i.e.* the smaller guerrilla groups.

Prokopis Papastratis: You mean that the British did not influence the Greek government-in-exile at all?
George Alexander: No. I mean that they had nothing to do with the selection of Papandreou to be prime minister. Once the King had selected him and Leeper had discussed matters with him and the policy he would follow was known to the British and had manifested itself in the Lebanon Charter, then the British gave him full support.
Prokopis Papastratis: On this particular point, on the selection of Papandreou, there is a telegram from Leeper to the FO saying that the King "hesitated to take the plunge, and I took it for him".
George Alexander: Yes, that's right. The King selected Papandreou but what the King said to Leeper was: "I'm afraid that, if I bring this man in on my own, he is going to be called the King's man and I don't want this to happen". Also there was the idea of throwing out Sophocles Venizelos who at that time, was unfortunately the leading bourgeois politician in Cairo. Therefore Leeper, knowing that the King wanted help on this from him, persuaded Venizelos to go. But the original selection was the King's.
Heinz Richter: Could you tell me exactly how Venizelos was forced out of office after the mutiny was crushed and they didn't need him any more? And then Papandreou, the "Trojan horse", it was his turn then. There is no doubt that Papandreou had agreed in advance to bring back the King.
George Kyrtsos: The questions we are dealing with are not only of historical but also of the most immediate political interest. I'd like to concentrate on the two contributions which most directly confront each other — George Alexander's and Thanasis Hajis'. In my opinion, George Alexander's paper is an excellent product of the dominant US ideology. *(Applause and some hissing).* For him, the anti-imperialist struggle of the Greek people does not exist, never existed. The problem of social progress is scaled down to a "communist plot". He did not offer any analysis of the concrete economic and social conditions, no analysis of the Greek communists' contribution to social progress during the crucial years we are examining. This kind of analysis shows the reactionary character of the dominant US ideology. What's good for General Motors is good for the USA. Why not also for Greece, Vietnam, Angola? At the same time, by over-simplifying the political process, George Alexander makes a primitive attempt to justify American imperialism, to justify the Truman doctrine, the military dictatorship and the continuing subversive imperialist activities of the US in the Mediterranean and in Greece. In opposition to this, Thanasis Hajis' paper succeeded in showing the contribution of the Communist Party and of the other progressive forces to the liberation struggle. He was able to identify the main contradictions of the period and to demonstrate the reactionary character of imperialist intervention. What is more, he has been able to establish a sense of historical continuity

which can be summed up in the phrase that he mentioned "EAM-ELAS — Polytechnic*" The struggle of the Greek people against the Greek bourgeoisie and the imperialist forces goes on. The struggle, of course, assumes different forms under different historical conditions but it will continue until the final objective is achieved. If we have difficulty in grasping this sense of continuity, the policy of the Karamanlis government which represents bourgeois and imperialist interests is a further proof. This government not only has a policy contrary to the interests of the working masses... (*Uproar in the auditorium:* "You are out of context", etc.) First, this government refuses to recognise the contribution of EAM-ELAS and other patriotic forces to the struggle for the liberation of our country. Secondly, it refuses to accept an unconditional return to Greece for tens of thousands of patriots whose only crime is that they opposed imperialist intervention. I therefore propose a resolution demanding that the Greek Government recognise the EAM-ELAS resistance and accept the unconditional return of the political refugees who live in the socialist countries *(Uproar in the auditorium)*. Mr. Chairman, I submit a resolution...

Chairman: I'm afraid I'm not prepared to accept a resolution at this point. You made a number of comments on George Alexander's paper. I think the best thing is to ask him whether he would like to reply. Also I know that Richard Clogg would like to make a point about that.

George Kyrtsos: I have the feeling that here we discuss as democrats and, in my view, the majority of democratic opinion in Greece supports the points I mentioned. I'd like to find out whether the audience wants to make a contribution in that direction.

Chairman: I think the purpose of this meeting was primarily historical, as an exchange of views and opinions and, if we attempt to put a resolution such as you suggest, it would almost certainly lead to an effective break-up of the meeting which I'd like to avoid. I feel the right course to take at this meeting is to carry on the discussion, especially as we have people who took part in the events concerned. There will, I think, be other more suitable forums for you to put the motion you are proposing.

George Alexander: You brought up so many points that I'll just choose a few. I don't think — in fact I'm sure I never said — that there was anything wrong with the communists pursuing power. I understand why they wanted to take power; because other political forces in Greece at that time were bankrupt. What I disagree with are arguments that the

---

* The massive demonstration by students at the Athens Polytechnic in November 1973 put down with slaughter by the first Junta dictatorship and immediately responsible for its fall. This allusion does not occur in Mr Hajis' translated text and may have been lost in translation of the subsequent discussion.

Communist Party wanted to restore a bourgeois parliamentary system in Greece or that KKE was some kind of social-democratic organisation. What I wanted to stress is that they wanted power and that, in critical times during World War II, they demanded those Ministries which would have given them complete power. Now there was no Centre in Greece at that time. It was either the Communists or the King. So I'll use that phrase which has sometimes not been understood and say that I sympathise with the communists when they say that they wanted power.
Dimitris Dimitrakos (interrupting): We don't care if you "sympathise".
George Alexander: O.K. I'll re-phrase it. My point is that I understand why they wanted to take power. I'm not saying whether this is a good or a bad thing, for them to have it or not. That is for people who have taken political positions to say. Now if you think that because I don't say whether it's good or bad, I reflect the "dominant US ideology," that is your opinion.
Richard Clogg: I'd like to make the point that, whatever else we are going to talk about this evening, we should not talk about US imperialism. About British imperialism may be. At the period George Alexander is talking about, the Americans were very much on the periphery of Greek affairs. They knew nothing, they cared very little and I think that it is wholly irrelevant to get into a discussion about US imperialism.
George Catephores: I have to raise again a few questions regarding military efficiency. I'd like to ask Brigadier Myers something. You say in your book* that ELAS was reluctant to participate in the Gorgopotamos operation. If we take it that far back, these were really early days and everybody was trying to learn the rules of this new game, so I don't know how much weight to place on these hesitations. But what I want to ask is: were there any hesitations on the side of Zervas, not in relation to Gorgopotamos, but earlier on? Whether Zervas hesitated to come out to the mountains, to fight? whether there was any hesitation on his side?
Brigadier Myers: One occasion I can remember early on when he was very obstinate and that was when I was trying to persuade him to sign the modified military agreement of June-July 1943 and become a member of the Joint GHQ with the ELAS members.
George Catephores: I am sorry — I was asking about before he became a guerrilla, whether he hesitated at that early stage?
Yanis Yanoulopoulos: We can make that question more specific. On what conditions did Zervas join the guerrillas?
George Catephores: Can we just state that Zervas was reluctant to take to the mountains, that he only did so under considerable British pressure? Is that a fact or not?
Brigadier Myers: I believe it is. I didn't know it until about 18 months

* see footnote to p.122

ago. It is very new to me. It did not affect my relations with him or his with me.

Richard Clogg: It did not affect the fighting capability of Zervas and EDES. It does not alter or in any way undermine the fact that in 1942 he was a very capable soldier, very willing to take part in sabotage operations, whilst ELAS was hesitant.

George Catephores: Right, right. I'll come to the hesitation of ELAS in a moment. But, before we come to that, we have established that someone who hesitates at some stage may become a very efficient soldier at a later stage. Now, to go on from there and question what you, Richard Clogg, said: that it would be nonsensical to let ELAS dominate and give the Germans a bloody fight because ELAS showed signs of hesitation over Gorgopotamos...

Richard Clogg: No, no. I didn't say that at all. What I said was that it would be nonsensical to ask Zervas to submit to ELAS on the grounds of greater military efficiency, of the greater fighting capability of ELAS.

George Catephores: Well, all right, of course, I am not suggesting that military efficiency was the criterion of the British Military Mission in the mountains. That was the point strongly underlined by Professor Hammond and I query that point. You are saying now that it would be nonsensical to ask Zervas to submit to ELAS on grounds of its superior military efficiency which you accept — or not?

Richard Clogg: I said that you could not ask Zervas, who had willingly, without hesitation, taken part in Gorgopotamos — although ELAS was reluctant, — to adhere to ELAS on the grounds of military efficiency. Can I put a question to you? Do you accept that ELAS was reluctant to take part in the Gorgopotamos operation?

George Catephores: Not on the evidence that I have read. Obviously I was not there and I cannot say. Brigadier Myers has first-hand knowledge and he has formed his own opinion. I can only read the books. I have not found any evidence of hesitation on the part of ELAS in joining the Gorgopotamos operation, unless it was a tactical hesitation of very short duration.

Richard Clogg: I think it could have been tactical in terms of orthodox communist theory. This would be perfectly reasonable for ELAS.

Chairman: George, we appreciate your Socratic approach in asking questions so as to elicit answers. But I think it's very time-consuming. Could you please summarise them so that other people can also have an opportunity to speak.

George Catephores: So, as I said in relation to Gorgopotamos, the only evidence I have is what I have read. Apart from Brigadier Myers' assessment, I have not read of this. The assessment that Nikiforos* gives does

---

* D. Dimitriou-Nikiforos, an ELAS participant in the Gorgopotamos operation; author of 'To Chroniko tou Gorgopotamou' 'Andartis sta vouna tis Roumelis' and other books published in Athens.

not indicate any hesitation on the part of ELAS.
Richard Clogg: Would you agree that, in the early years, in 1942, it was EAM's policy (and it was fully in accord with orthodox communist theory) to concentrate the effort, the liberation struggle, in the towns rather than in the mountains. This would be a perfectly valid explanation for ELAS' hesitation to take part. It makes sense, nothing to be ashamed about, a simple fact.
George Catephores: Maybe you are right that this was the case in the first months and even for a very long period. In my own opinion it was an issue that was never resolved in the minds of the communist leadership — which was the preferable way to fight. But that does not imply, Richard Clogg, that those who are in the mountains are instructed not to fight. Maybe we don't send everybody to the mountains but those who are there, are there to fight the Germans, not to drag their feet.
Richard Clogg: We can accept that we are going to agree that there are contradictions.
George Catephores: I don't want to give anyone the impression that I agree. At least, as far as I have read, I cannot agree that ELAS was hesitating. It might be interesting to ask Brigadier Myers to give us a soldier's assessment of the relative contribution of ELAS and EDES to the blowing-up at Gorgopotamos. I don't want an immediate answer. I won't press it but I want to raise it. Now, I think it has been said that the communists were more successful because they were able organisers, trained during the Metaxas dictatorship to work and organise underground. I'd say with all due respect that I find this, well *kolokythia** *(Laughter)* because, under Metaxas, they were swept away completely by the Security forces and didn't show any remarkable ability to survive that. They did not survive it well at all.
Chairman: George, there are lots of people who would like to speak. Could you bring your remarks to a close, please?
George Catephores: To bring my remarks to a close, I'd say that the real strength of ELAS was not in any technical capacity of its organisers but in the new type of army, the new type of popular activity which they organised and which allowed the masses to develop a free initiative which had been frustrated by the official Greek State, by the Metaxas State, the pre-Metaxas State, the officers, the officials, the petty officials, all those sitting on the backs of the Greek people and particularly of the peasantry, who had not allowed them to develop their creative initiative. The strength of ELAS was that the communist leadership had confidence in the masses and allowed them to develop this creative initiative and, if they had got a free hand all over Greece, they would have developed this initiative to an even greater extent. There was no question of the people turning against ELAS, even if the

---

*   pumpkins. A Greek expression for "nonsense".

other groups had been forcibly integrated. I think one can strongly support this point as far as the German Occupation and the maximisation of the fight against the Germans is concerned. After that, of course, some are communists, some are anti-communist; some are socialists, some are liberal democrats and we all have our different opinions about the relative value of regimes. But I think, if we are limited to the period of the German Occupation and we ask the question how the struggle could be maximised and by what means it was maximised by EAM-ELAS, I think it is clear that the strength of EAM-ELAS was in its ability to free the creative initiative of the masses and it would have freed this to a greater extent had it not been for the British Military Mission holding it back. *(Applause)*.

Roussos Koundouros: I remember, after a long session at King's College, 3 or 4 years ago, Brigadier Myers saying "In the end we brought Zervas to the mountains". I wonder whether he will repeat this statement. And a question to Professor Hammond: how will he account for the figures Papastratis gave for relative supplies and that not during the clashes between ELAS and EDES?

Professor Hammond: What were the dates he gave?

Prokopis Papastratis: From the end of the Lebanon Conference. The telegram from Cairo to London is dated 29 June.

Brigadier Myers: Of course, when I came into the field, Zervas was already there. So it's knowledge I acquired afterwards and what we did to get Zervas to the mountains had nothing to do with me. I am told, and I am ready to believe it, that we tried over quite a period of time to persuade the British authorities through our agent in Athens to get Zervas to take to the mountains and that he was unwilling. We wanted a resistance movement that would fight and we did not know very much, if anything, about ELAS in those days. It was as simple as that, I believe. We wanted a soldier whom we could rely on in the mountains and it was not a very light decision because, if you were well-known, your family were liable to be arrested by the enemy — you had to make arrangements for them. In fact, he took his brother and, I think, his wife to the mountains with him, to the Valtos area. But he had hesitations and in the end, I am told on reliable authority, the British threatened to tell the Germans about his offer to go to the mountains unless he did so. And he was given some money to take to the mountains. That I believe to be the truth.

Richard Clogg: Could I make a very minor correction to what Brigadier Myers said? Zervas was threatened with exposure to the Germans, not directly by the British but by "Prometheus" (Captain Koutsoyannopoulos). Whether he was acting on his own initiative or under instructions from Cairo I don't know. But there is no doubt that Zervas had to be strongly encouraged, to put it mildly. *(Laughter)* May I just throw in another point which might perhaps clear the waters a little? That the British brought Zervas to the mountains has been presumed to imply that his primary function was to resist ELAS. I'd like to point out that SOE in the Middle East was giving gold sovereigns in substantial quantities to EAM as early as December 1941, *i.e.* within 3 months of its foundation. This is, I think quite an interesting point.

Professor Hammond: With regard to the period from May 1944 to June, when ELAS received 31 tons, the *capetans* 6½ tons and Zervas 132 tons, the answer is briefly this. After the destruction of EKKA, supplies to ELAS were stopped for a longish period. Secondly we were bringing in Raiding Support Regiments* and also American support regiments through Epirus. They landed on the coast of Epirus and we had to pass them through the German lines which ran from Yannina. Therefore it was important to get a lot of stuff there which was used by these Raiding Support Regiments. That accounts, I think, for the main part of the discrepancy.

Roussos Koundouros: This discrepancy is completely out of proportion, that's my point. It's out of proportion.

Professor Hammond: It was in terms of military objectives.

Roussos Koundouros: Out of proportion to the relative strengths of ELAS and EDES.

Richard Clogg: You must put yourself in the place of the policy-makers, of the British military authorities in Cairo. In April 1944, EKKA was forcibly dissolved and its leader, Psarros was brutally murdered. I think everybody in this room will accept that this took place and that the perpetrators of the crime were members of ELAS. Now, whether this crime was authorised by the EAM Central Committee, this is another question entirely. Nevertheless the murder is a fact, a historical fact which we accept now and which the authorities in Cairo knew at the time. Now, when you hear of the cold-blooded murder of Greek patriots of impeccable democratic credentials – in no circumstances could Psarros be described even remotely as a fascist, collaborator or anything else like that – you are suspicious of the organisation that you think responsible for his murder and for the dissolution of his band. What do you do? The only thing you do is to cut off supplies and that's what happened. It's only logical.

George Petrochilos: We have heard from a number of speakers that ELAS was reluctant to engage in operations against the Occupation forces. Now, can anyone, please, give us the number of Occupation troops in Greece during those years; – not in terms of divisions because I understand that there was a difference in the numbers of men in German and in British divisions. If the actual number of Occupation forces was a significant one, then obviously ELAS which was controlling about four-fifths of the country, should at least get the credit for holding them there. If, of course, the number was insignificant, then one cannot talk of resistance.

---

* see footnote to p.113

Brigadier Myers: The facts are as follows. By the time I left Greece in summer 1943, if I remember rightly, the overall standing strength of ELAS, not counting any village reserves who had weapons hidden away and occasionally came out to give support, was in the order of 15,000 *andartes** and the permanent strength of Zervas at that time was about 5,000. I may be wrong but that is what I remember.

George Petrochilos: What was the strength of the Occupation forces?

Brigadier Myers: That is a much more difficult question for me to answer because, frankly, I don't remember now. I doubt if I ever knew. We were not interested. I personally, as Head of Mission, was concerned not so much with the number of German troops we were tying down as with the sabotage operations we were required to prepare. For instance, the "Animals" operation** took us 3 months to prepare for. I was given the first warning about the proposed invasion of Sicily in January & it took place in July. I immediately started preparations which occupied me fully as a priority military job for months. So I'm afraid I cannot answer your question. I'm not trying to evade it.

George Petrochilos: My attention has been drawn to the book 'O ELAS' by General Sarafis,† according to which there were 300,000 Occupation troops in Greece. Of course, after the Italians capitulated and only the Germans and Bulgarians remained, this was reduced to 180,000. However the Occupation troops included some excellent German divisions like the Edelweiss. This shows that ELAS, far from being reluctant to engage in operations were doing all they could and as a result very good German divisions were being tied down.

Heinz Richter: Let me make a statement. In Greece there was one good division, the 22nd, stationed on Crete. In Attica the 11th Luftwaffen Felddivision which was something rather particular. The two other divisions, the 104 Jägerdivision and the 117 Jägerdivision, were second-rate. Two more divisions, the 1 Panzerdivision and the Gebirgsdivision, came in for a few weeks in 1943 and went out again. And there were some fortress regiments (the 966 and 967 Festungsregiment), mainly elderly men (Landesschützen) on guard duties. The 4 SS Polizei-Panzer-Grenadier-Division in reality consisted of two police regiments. That means altogether roughly 50-70,000 Germans.

George Petrochilos: Sarafis gives 100,000 Germans and other nationalities in addition. What we are talking about is the total number of foreign Occupation forces in Greece and whether this number would have been smaller had ELAS not been there. Now, if ELAS with 50,000 men managed to hold down 300,000 Occupation troops which could have been used elsewhere, the contention that ELAS was reluctant to

---

* see footnote to page 118
** see footnote to page 118
† 'O ELAS' by its c-in-c. Maj. Gen. Stefanos Sarafis, *Athens*, 1946. To be published in an English edition under the title 'ELAS: Greek Resistance Army' by the Merlin Press, London, 1980.

engage in operations against the Occupation forces is not very convincing.
Richard Clogg: But they were really fairly low-grade, these Occupation troops, both Italians and Germans.
Yanis Yanoulopoulos: I'd like to ask a very brief question about something which has always puzzled me. I think Professor Hammond is the only one competent to answer it. Was any member of the Mission aware of the fact − for we now know it's a fact − that Zervas actually concluded a pact with the Germans? If the answer is "no" I'd like to know why not? If the answer is "yes", what was done about it?
Professor Hammond: I said we did not know of any agreement between Zervas and the Germans. There was a report to that effect by ELAS but whether it was ever proved I don't know. I think there were also reports about ELAS. I remember a high-up member of ELAS informing me that they were starting a Free German movement towards the end. I had great suspicions.
George Yanoulopoulos: But now we know it's a fact. How do you explain its being kept a secret? Doesn't it surprise you?
Professor Hammond: Individual officers were concerned with their own units. There were liaison officers with individual units. The 75 officers in Greece didn't all get together in one place and talk. We did not know if it was true.
George Yanoulopoulos: In the preface he wrote for the Greek edition of *Apple of Discord*,* Woodhouse says it is true but he didn't know.
Professor Hammond: If he didn't know, no one else could.
Question from the auditorium: Professor Hammond, you said that the Mission in Greece was trying to pursue a policy of even-handedness with regard to the resistance movements. Whenever ELAS attacked other movements, you withheld British arms. My question is this: did that apply to the other side? Because I suppose EDES retaliated.
Professor Hammond: I think I've already replied to that.
Dimitris Dimitrakos: I'd like to make a few comments. They concern mainly what I heard from Thanasis Hajis and from Professor Hammond. If they'd like to reply, they are welcome; if not it doesn't matter. I'll start from what Thanasis Hajis said about the analysis of the probable international situation that would emerge after the war made by the KKE Central Committee. I think the importance of this analysis was not duly emphasised. He told us they were trying to guess what the interests of the Soviet Union were so as to serve these best. That's interesting. What I find even more interesting is the dichotomy between those who said that after the war there would probably be two camps reproducing the class conflict, as it were at a world level; and the others who said "no − everyone will be united". In a strange way, in a contradictory way, in a dialectical way, both are confirmed. The first

---

*   English edition, Hutchinson & Co., London. N.D. (1948)

is confirmed in the struggle that is still with us to-day since the end of the war; the second in so far as we can say that there is also a world of co-existence. What I'd like to emphasise is the way in which, within the Greek context, they were reproducing within themselves a world conflict that was going on, that was going to go on. This shows that it was not just a fight between political factions, between Mediterranean politicians and sensible Anglo-Saxons who put themselves in as arbitrators. The struggle in Greece had a world significance and proportions. This brings me to another point, made by Thanasis Skouras, which I found very pertinent, and also by another young man who has gone now, about the continuity between politics and military operations. The Clausewitzian continuity, war being the continuation of politics, implies also that politics is another way of continuing war and this is something we are witnessing to-day. This is the very antithesis of Professor Hammond's analysis when he saw a clear distinction between military operations and political considerations, between British military operations and Greek politics and these again being completely dissociated from the objectives of British foreign policy and the strategy of Churchillian foreign policy. I think the political considerations of British foreign policy in general determined the military operations in Greece and also throw a meaningful light on these military actions. Consequently, even if the British Military Mission formally played the arbiter between warring Greek factions, the stakes involved were much larger than the word "faction" implies, for they had their consequence in a world conflict. In 1944 we were not involved in a War of the Roses between the Houses of Lancaster and York. It was much more important. Britain played the role of "arbiter"...

Professor Hammond (interrupting): Zervas' House and Aris' House, you might say. *(Laughter)*

Dimitris Dimitrakos:... Although even this role of arbiter was debunked by the contributions from Heinz Richter and Thanasis Hajis. Even if we accepted this, the essential is not the role of the arbiter between warring factions. I think, first of all, they were not simply political factions and, secondly, that the explanation of British military actions in Greece is given by Britain's foreign policy objectives seen in a world context, not British magnanimity, not Churchillian sentiments "what we owe to Greece because she was our ally" and so forth. This, of course, is not to say that I accuse British foreign policy of not being magnanimous. It is only to demonstrate once more the separation of ethics and politics which both Aristotle and Macchiavelli have noted before us. Emotionalism always gets mobilised on political issues and tends to confuse the issue, whether it comes from right-wing or from left-wing speakers.

Professor Hammond: On what you said about Thanasis Hajis saying that the KKE was eager to know what it should do for the Soviet Union, could I first say that there is no doubt that, if they had had

their way, we would have had a Soviet Union in Greece. We saw it happening in Albania. We saw it happening initially in Yugoslavia. I think there is no doubt this is what would have happened.
Tape recordings end at this point
Chairman: Though there are several people who still wish to make a contribution, I must regretfully bring the Conference to a close, I am sure I express the views of all of you here present when I say that the Conference has been an undoubted success: a success due both to the quality and interest of the presentations and to the frankness of the questioners and contributors from the floor. Another key factor in the success of the Conference has been the presence amongst our speakers and audience of many people who participated in the events we have been discussing. Their presence has been invaluable and we are indeed grateful to them for being here with us. I would like to conclude by thanking all the speakers for their stimulating presentations and also the organisers who have brought us all together. I very much hope that this will be the first of more conferences of this kind dealing with aspects of Greece's recent past.

Appendix

Mr. Hajis has submitted the following supplementary question to Brigadier Myers:

Brigadier Myers, Head of the British Military Mission in the Greek mountains during the first stage, assures us that he was fair and impartial in his attitude to all the guerrilla organisations and that the only thing which concerned him was their military activity against the conquerors. I will not cite published evidence which has revealed certain actions of his against EAM-ELAS. But there is one very clear document, Report No. 85/4 AS of 12 August 1943 which was first published in the US and frequently thereafter in Greece (*see* Ph. Grigoriadis 'To Andartiko)* and has never been disclaimed by Brigadier Eddie who signed it. This report states categorically that he gave instructions to his British and Greek subordinates to 'undermine the work of EAM and ELAS' and that the British agents 'have a right and a duty to denounce the EAM-ELAS leaders to the Occupation authorities and to assist in securing the arrest of EAM-ELAS agents, so that, when the moment comes, these organisations should not be in a position to damage British interests. In this connection, the EDES organisation has already done much. It has denounced to Colonel Dertilis and to the Minister Tavoularis several active members of EAM and ELAS who are now in the hands of the Germans and of the Occupation authorities.' About EKKA he wrote 'The Leader of this group Colonel Psarros is honest and absolutely consistent in his promises to us. His political advisers, Kapsalopoulos and Kartalis, incessantly demand financial aid and I do not know whether they are making good use of the sums they receive, as I learn that great amounts are spent by them on their private businesses. However, both of them have so far been working for the dissolution of ELAS'.

The extracts in quotation marks are from the report by Brigadier

---

* published in leaflet form under the title 'Praise and Perfidy: British Sentiments and Tory Actions' by the Greek-American Council, *New York*, N.D. (1945); Ph. Grigoriadis, 'To Antartiko, ELAS, EDES, EKKA – 5/42, *Athens*, 1964. 5v.

APPENDIX 135

Myers. I think it would serve the cause of historical truth if he would either confirm or deny the geniuneness of this document* since so far he has not done so.

Brigadier Myers has replied as follows:—

Reply to Mr. Hajis' Question

So far as I can remember, this is the first time I have ever heard of the existence of "Strictly Confidential" report No 85/4AS, dated 12 August, 1943, referred to now by Mr Hajis and apparently attributed to me. I denounce it without hesitation as a blatant, inaccurate and malicious forgery.

The forger was apparently unaware that on 12 August 1943 I was in Cairo, with an *andarte* delegation from the Greek mountains. EAM-ELAS had recently co-operated with the Allied Forces in the Middle East in carrying out widespread sabotage in conjunction with the recently completed invasion of Sicily. The sentence in the above mentioned document in which I am supposed to have written "I hope to be able to bring them (ELAS) to the point of putting out the necessary orders for the carrying out of sabotage" bears no relation to the actual situation on 12 August 1943.

Moreover, being in Cairo there was no necessity for me to write any letter to GHQ, Middle East on such diverse matters as in this concocted letter. In fact, at no time did I ever write any letters to GHQ Middle East from the mountains. My reports were invariably sent to SOE HQ in Cairo, in cript sentences suitable for being encyphered and transmitted by wireless. I never sent any written reports by hand from Greece to anyone.

I never received any instructions from my superiors which required me to act in any two-faced underhand way.

Apart from the fact that several of the Greek personalities mentioned in this document were at the time unknown to me — and I was therefore unqualified to report on them, as many people now know, the style of writing and phraseology in the forged document is not mine.

Copies of the reports I wrote whilst in Cairo and London during

---

* The Editor would like to add that, when she discussed this document with her late husband, Major-General Stefanos Sarafis, military commander of ELAS, he expressed the opinion that it could not be genuine since "though others might have written thus, it was not in character for Brigadier Eddie". Its appearance in the Appendix to the German edition of General Sarafis' book 'O ELAS' published under the title 'In den Bergen von Hellas' by Deutscher Militärverlag, *Berlin*, 1964, occurred without her knowledge and she subsequently expressed her regret to the publishers that an otherwise creditable edition should have been disfigured by the use of a forged document, where previous consultation could have prevented this.

the summer of 1943 can now be studied in the military history archives of King's College, London University. None will be found with any remotely similar reference number to 85/4AS, which, along with the whole of the letter, I denounce as a fabrication.

E.C.W. Myers

Glossary

BMM	British Military Mission
CC	Central Committee
EAM	Ethniko Apelftherotiko Metopo (National Liberation Front)
EDES	Ethnikos Dimokratikos Ellinikos Syndesmos (National Democratic Greek League)
EKKA	Ethniki kai Koinoniki Apeleftherosis (National and Social Liberation)
ELAS	Ethnikos Laikos Apeleftherotikos Stratos (National Popular Liberation Army)
EPON	Ethniki Panelladiki Organosis Neolaias (National Panhellenic Youth Organisation). EAM's Youth Movement.
KKE	Kommounistiko Komma Elladas (Greek Communist Party)
PAO	Panelliniki Apeleftheriki Organosis (Panhellenic Liberation Organisation)
PEEA	Politiki Epitropi Ethnikis Apeleftherosis (Political Committee for National Liberation)
SIS	Special Intelligence Service
SOE	Special Operations Executive
YVE	Yperaspistai Voreiou Ellados (Defenders of Northern Greece)

The following presented papers or took part in discussion

Alexander, George. PhD. King's College, University of London.

Alexiou, Christos. Lecturer in Modern Greek, University of Brimingham.

Barker, Elisabeth. Writer and broadcaster on Southeast European affairs. Author of 'British Policy in South-East Europe in the Second World War'. *London,* 1976.

Carratt, Chris A. An American (of Greek origin) who joined Force 133 in Greece during the early stages of the guerrilla war.

Catephores, George. Lecturer in Economics, University College, University of London.

Clogg, Richard. Lecturer in Greek History, King's College, University of London. Editor (with Phyllis Auty) of 'British Policy towards Wartime Resistance in Yugoslavia and Greece'. *London,* 1974. Author of 'A Short History of Modern Greece'. *London,* 1979.

Cookridge, the late E.H. Writer on Second World War history. Author of 'Secrets of the British Secret Service.' *London,* 1948.

CONTRIBUTORS

Dimitrakos, Dimitris. Lecturer in Politics, Rheims University.

Doganis, Rigas. Professor of Transport Studies, Polytechnic of Central London.

Dragoumis, Markos. Press Councillor, Greek Embassy.

Fleischer, Hagen. PhD. Free University, Berlin.

Hajis, Thanasis. Secretary-General of EAM 1941-4. Author of 'I Nikifora Epanastasi pou hathike' (The Victorious Revolution That Was Lost'), *Athens*, 3v. 1977-80.

Hammond, Professor Nicholas, F.B.A. Professor of Greek, University of Bristol. Wartime liaison officer in Northern Greece. Acting Head of British Military Mission 1944.

Kedros, Andreas. Writer on Greek Resistance history. Author of 'La Résistance Grecque' *Paris*, 1966. 'Peuple Roi.' *Paris*, 1952.

Kotsis, Spyros. Former senior Police Director. Author of 'Midas 614'. *Athens*, 1976.

Koundouros, Roussos. Part-time Lecturer in Sociology, Brunel University.

Kyrtsos, George. Post-graduate student. London School of Economics.

Myers, Brigadier E.C.W. CBE, DSO. Head of the British Military Mission to Greece 1942-43. Author of 'Greek Entanglement'. *London*, 1955.

Papastratis, Prokopis. PhD., Research Associate at the Academy of Athens Institute for Modern Greek History Studies.

Pesmazoglou, Vasilis. Economics Research Assistant, Thames Polytechnic.

Petrochilos, George. Principal Lecturer in Economics, Lanchester Polytechnic.

Richter, Heinz. PhD. Heidelberg. Author of 'Griechenland zwischen Revolution und Konterrevolution (1936-1946)'. *Frankfurt*, 1973; Greek edition, *Athens* 1975. Researcher for Deutsche Forschungsgemeinschaft Bonn, 1976-9.

Skouras, Thanasis. PhD., Head of Political Economy Dept. N.E. London Polytechnic.

Svoronos, Professor Nicos. Head of Department Ecole Pratique des Hautes Etudes, Paris. Author of 'Histoire de la Grèce Moderne'. *Paris*, 1972; Greek edition, *Athens*, 1976.

Sweet-Escott, Bickham. Wartime senior SOE operative. Author of 'Greece: A Political and Economic Survey 1939-1953'. *London*, 1954; 'Baker Street Irregular' *London*, 1965.

Yanoulopoulos, George. Greek Section BBC.

Yanoulopoulos, Yanis. PhD. Lecturer in Modern Greek History. University of Crete.

Editorial Note: In the papers, transliteration from Greek and footnote notation follow the contributor's own usage.

Index

This index, which is selective, also gives brief descriptions of the Greek personalities mentioned in the book.

Abwehr (German Counter-Intelligence). 52, 54.
Albania. 15-16, 18, 29, 45, 67, 68, 119, 133; Albanian campaign. 9, 53.
Allied Military Mission (the BMM after it was joined by the US). 38, 94.
Anastasiadis, Stergios (member of KKE Political Bureau). 77.
Anglo-Greek Committee (Cairo). 33.
'Animals' Operation (to cover Allied landing in Sicily). 35, 52, 118, 130, 135.
Apollo (Greek pro-allied espionage group). 93, 94, 96, 97, 107.
Argyropoulos, Colonel Archimidis. 115.
Aris *see* Velouchiotis, Aris
Asia Minor disaster (1922). 13.
ASO (Left-wing military organisation within the Greek Middle East forces). 98.
Asopos viaduct. 91-2, 96.
Atlantic Charter. 57.

Bakirjis, Colonel Euripides (Republican officer, later Major-General; joined ELAS and PEEA). 32.
Bakouros, Pavlos. 94, 103.
Balkan Federation. 17-18.
Bank of Greece. 89.
Barnes, Colonel Tom (British liaison officer). 37, 38.
Bathgate, Major (British liaison officer). 85, 86, 87.
BBC. 98, 115, 122.
Bevan, Aneurin. 79.
Bevin, Ernest. 29-30.

Bouras, Pavlos (Chief of Athens Police 1945). 104.
British Military Mission (BMM). 23, 33-4, 55, 56, 58, 74, 108-9, 112, 113, 114, 115, 116, 117, 119-20, 128, 131, 134.
Bulgaria. 16, 17, 18, 26-7, 28, 29, 30, 45, 63.

Cadogan, Alexander. 21.
Canellopoulos, Panayotis (politician of the Right-Centre, Vice-Premier in National Unity Government). 32.
Caserta Conference & Agreement 12, 40, 51, 56, 58, 59, 73, 86.
Casey, R.G. (Minister of State for the Middle East). 89.
Chrysochoöu, Colonal Athanasios (wartime Inspector of N. Greece prefectures). 115-116.
Churchill, Winston. 10, 11, 15, 18-19, 20-6, 27-9, 35, 36, 40, 53-6, 57, 58, 59, 60, 61, 71, 79, 80, 81, 83-5, 86-7, 88, 89, 90, 98, 99, 101n., 113, 122, 132.
City, The (influence of). 81, 88-9.
Civil War (1947-9). 9, 59, 79.
Communist Party of Greece *see* KKE.

Damaskinos, Archbishop of Athens (later Regent of Greece). 20, 21, 28-9, 36, 64, 82, 90, 94, 105.
December 1944 clashes. 9, 10, 22, 28, 50-1, 59, 72, 78-90, 113.
Demobilisation of guerrillas. 43-4, 83, 87-8.
Dertilis, Colonel V. 134.
Dodecanese. 16, 71.
Dragoumis, Filippos (Foreign Minister in National Unity Government). 28.

INDEX

Drosos, George (journalist). 92.

EAM and EAM-ELAS. 9, 10, 11, 12, 17, 18, 19, 20, 21, 24, 25, 26, 27, 28, 29, 32-3, 34-6, 37-40, 43, 44, 45, 46, 47, 48, 50, 52-3, 54, 55, 56, 57-9, 61, 63, 67, 68-70, 71-2, 73, 74, 75, 76, 77, 78, 82, 84, 85, 86, 87, 92, 93, 95, 97-8, 107, 109, 112, 113, 114, 116, 117, 119, 120, 121, 124, 127, 128, 129, 134-5.

Eden, Anthony. 12, 15-18, 19, 20, 21, 23-5, 26, 27, 28, 29, 39, 40, 54, 60, 83.

EDES. 10, 12, 32, 33, 34, 35, 36, 37, 38, 43, 44, 52-3, 55, 58, 74, 87, 91, 108, 112, 113, 114, 117, 120, 121, 126, 127, 128, 131, 134.

Edmonds, Lt. Colonel Arthur (British liaison officer). 96.

Eggs, Major. *nom-de-guerre* of Professor Nicholas Hammond, *q.v.*

EKKA. 10, 21, 33, 37, 38-9, 70, 74, 108, 112, 113, 114, 121, 129, 134.

El Alamein. 55, 118.

ELAS. 10, 19, 20, 21, 26, 27, 28, 32-4, 36-40, 43, 44, 53, 54, 56, 61, 67, 69-70, 71, 72, 73, 76, 77, 78, 79, 85, 86, 87, 88, 89, 90, 91, 92, 98, 106, 108, 109-110, 111, 112, 113, 114, 115, 117, 119, 120, 121, 122, 125-6, 127-8, 129, 130, 131, 134-5. *See* EAM-ELAS.

Elections of 1946. 29, 75.

EPON. 67.

Ethniki Drasis (Right-wing nationalist organisation). 92, 94.

Eudes, Dominique (writer). 105.

Evert, Colonel Angelos (wartime Chief of Athens Police). 94, 104n.

Foreign Office (FO). 10, 16, 18, 25, 32, 33, 34, 35, 36, 37, 39, 40, 73, 82, 84, 87, 89, 93, 96, 97, 99, 105, 115, 120, 122, 123.

"Freedom" (Salonica liberation movement). 66.

Gallacher, William. 79.

Georgatos, Angelos (wartime Mayor of Athens). 93-4, 97, 102n., 103.

George II (King of Greece). 10, 18-19, 20-1, 25, 29, 32, 33, 34, 35, 36, 40, 46, 47, 54-5, 57, 58, 60, 61, 71, 81, 84, 85, 93, 106, 109-10, 113, 121, 122-3, 125.

German Occupation forces, (strength of). 129-30.

Gestapo. 94, 96, 97.

Gorgopotamos bridge. 33, 118, 122, 125-6, 127.

Greenwood, Arthur. 79.

Gusev, Feodor (wartime Soviet ambassador in London). 24-5, 26.

Hambro's Bank. 88.

Hammond, Professor Nicholas under *nom-de-guerre* Eggs. 116.

Harriman, Averell. 27.

Harris, Percy. 79.

Hitler, Adolf. 11, 15, 16, 52, 63, 65, 93, 94, 97, 99, 102n., 103, 104.

House of Commons. 90.

Hoxha, Enver. 110.

HQME (Heaquarters Middle East). 115, 116, 135.

Hull, Cordell. 25, 26, 56.

Hungary. 26, 28.

Iatridis, Professor John. 80.

IDEA (secret military organisation). 79.

'Ill met by moonlight' Operation. 118.

India (route to). 10, 53.

Ioanidis, Yannis (member of KKE Central Committee). 48, 49.

Ionian Bank. 88.

Jellicoe, Lord. 74.

Joint GHQ (Joint Guerrilla Command). 34-5, 52, 114, 116, 119, 125.

Junta (The Colonels' dictatorial regime 1967-74). 57, 79n., 89.

Kapsalopoulos, Apostolos (politician involved with EKKA). 134.

Karamanlis' Government. 124.

Karayiorgis, Kostas (journalist, EAM representative with Thessaly ELAS). 115.

Kartalis, George (politician of the Centre-Left, political adviser to EKKA). 38, 134.

Kerr, Archibald Clark. 23.

Kikitsas (*nom-de-guerre* of Sarantis Protopappas, ELAS capetan in Macedonia). 115, 199.

KKE (Greek Communist Party). 10, 11, 12, 29, 32, 40, 43-5, 46, 47, 48, 49, 50-1, 56, 64-5, 66-7, 68, 71, 73-5, 76-7, 80, 82, 98, 107, 109, 121, 123, 125, 131, 132.

Kousoulas, Professor D. George. 80, 111.
Koutsoyannopoulos, Captain *see* Prometheus.
Kyrtatos, Nikolaos. 92, 94, 95, 103.

Labour Party (British). 89.
Lake Copais Company. 88.
Lazaridis, K. (trade unionist). 87.
Lebanon Conference and Agreement (Charter). 12, 24, 25, 39-40, 44, 46, 48-50, 56, 73, 75, 85, 122, 123, 128.
Leeper, Reginald (British ambassador to the Greek Government in exile & later British ambassador in Greece). 19, 21, 23, 28, 34, 36, 37, 39, 82-3, 85, 86, 88, 89, 123.
Liberal Party (British). 79.
Liberal Party (Greek). 45, 83, 87.
Loos, Colonel R. (Chief of German Secret Military Police in the Balkans). 93-5, 99 103-5.

McIntyre (British liaison officer). 103.
McNeil, William Hardy (post-war US military attaché in Greece). 80.
Macedonia. 15, 17, 27, 29, 66, 68, 77, 111, 114, 116, 121.
Mahler, Dr. Julius (writer). 105.
Markos *see* Vafiadis, Markos.
Maule, Henry (writer). 80.
Mercourios (Salonica military resistance group). 66.
Metaxas, General John (dictator of Greece 1936-41). 10, 32, 54, 55, 57, 58, 60, 61, 64, 75, 81, 84, 110, 114, 121, 127.
Michael, King of Romania. 26.
Molotov, Vyacheslav. 17, 19, 20, 22-3, 24, 26, 28.
Morton, Bob (British liaison officer). 91, 103.
Moscow Conference & Agreement. 12, 17, 19-20, 56, 86.
Mousterakis, Colonel Yannis (later a divisional commander in ELAS). 115, 116.
"Mutiny" in Greek Middle East forces. 21-2, 39, 44, 46-7, 55, 56, 85, 123.
Myers, Brigadier Eddie (Head of British Military Mission 1942-3). 33, 34, 36, 55, 84, 103, 110, 128, 134-5.

National Bands. 34.

National Council (parliament of Free Greece). 75.
National Solidarity (Red Cross of the Resistance). 66.
National Unity Government. 12, 26, 38, 39-40, 43, 56, 113.
Neubacher, H. (German Plenipotentiary for S.E. Europe). 93, 94, 105-6.
Nikiforos (*nom-de-guerre* of D. Dimitriou, ELAS capetan). 126.
'Noah's Ark' Operation. 117, 122.
Novikov, Nikolai (Soviet ambassador in Cairo). 40.

Orestis (*nom-de-guerre* of Andreas Mountrichas, ELAS capetan). 92.
OSS (Office of Strategic Services. US Intelligence). 98.
'Overlord' Operation. 24.

PAO (ambivalent "resistance" organisation in N. Greece). 114-6, 119.
Papadopoulos, Colonel George (Junta dictator 1967-73). 79.
Papandreou, George (National Unity Government Prime Minister). 10, 23, 24, 25, 26, 27, 28, 39, 43, 44, 47-9, 50, 56, 58, 71, 75, 82, 83, 85, 86, 87, 88, 91, 113, 122, 123.
PAS (coalition of Athens nationalist groups). 92.
Pearson Group. 88.
PEEA. 21, 26, 39, 40, 44, 45, 47, 48, 49, 50, 56, 75, 113.
Petimezas, Iraklis (politician of the non-EAM Left). 86.
Plaka Conference. 38-9.
Plastiras, General Nikolaos (Republican officer in foreign exile, later Prime Minister). 86.
Plebiscite (or referendum) on the monarchy. 18-19, 20, 29, 35, 36, 45, 55, 57, 84, 110, 121.
Plumbidis, Nikolaos (member of KKE Central Committee). 65, 77.
Popov, Colonel Grigori (Head of Soviet Military Mission to ELAS). 26, 28, 40.
Prometheus (code-name of Captain Koutsoyannopoulos working for British Intelligence in Athens). 117, 128.
Psarros, Colonel Dimitris (Republican officer, military commander of EKKA). 34, 53, 56, 58, 60, 66, 129, 134.

INDEX

Public Record Office. 83, 85, 87, 88, 99, 122.
Pyromaglou, Komninos (politician of the Centre-Left, second-in-command of EDES). 33, 38.

Quebec Conference. 19.

Raiding Support Regiments. 113, 129.
Rallis, John (third collaborationist Prime Minister). 114.
Red Army. 26, 69, 70, 95.
Referendum *see* Plebiscite.
Resistance (non-recognition of), 53, 124; *see also* Supplying of
Romania. 17, 22-5, 26, 27-8, 29, 56, 95, 105.
Roosevelt, Franklin D. 10, 19, 20, 23, 24-5, 27, 28, 36, 55, 56, 79.
Rousos, Petros (member of KKE Central Committee). 49-50, 75, 76.
Roussos, George (briefly Prime Minister in 1944). 47.

Samariniotis, Vasilis. *nom-de-guerre* of Andreas Tzimas, *q.v.*
Sarafis, Colonel Stefanos (Republican officer, later Major-General; military commander of ELAS). 34. 113, 130, 135n.
Scheiben (first German Governor of Athens). 63.
Schürmann, Karl. (German officer). 94, 95, 103, 104.
Scobie, Lt. General Ronald (c-in-c of British forces in Greece 1944). 27, 56, 83, 113.
Security Battalions (anti-resistance units raised by the Greek Collaborationist Government). 59, 72, 91, 107, 114, 115, 117, 122.
Seferiadis, A. (leader of a resistance group). 120.
Sheppard, Colonel Rufus (British liaison officer). 115, 120.
Siantos, George (Acting Secretary-General of KKE). 45, 48, 50, 75, 77, 90, 110, 111.
Siphnaios, Panayotis (leader of Ethniki Drasis group). 92, 95.
SIS (Special Intelligence Service). 89.
Smuts, General Jan Christian. 18-19, 20-1.
Sobolev, Arkady (Soviet Assistant Foreign Minister). 16.
SOE (Special Operations Executive). 18, 26, 32, 33, 34, 37, 55, 91, 93, 94, 95, 96, 97, 99, 106, 116, 117, 120, 129, 135.
Sofoulis, Themistocles (leader of Greek Liberal Party, later Prime Minister). 45-6, 83, 87-8.
Sophianopoulos, John (politician of the non-EAM Left, Foreign Minister in 1945). 28.
Soviet Military Mission. 10, 23, 26, 51, 56, 58, 76, 108, 110, 113.
Speer, Albert (German Armaments Minister). 99.
Spheres of influence policy (also described as the percentage agreement). 10, 12, 19-20, 24-8, 56-7, 76, 81, 85, 86, 98.
Stalin, Joseph. 10, 12, 15-19, 25, 27-8, 29, 30, 56, 58, 98.
Stärker, Rudolf (German diplomat). 94, 95, 99, 105.
State Department. 25.
Stavrianos, Professor L.G. 80.
Stawell, General (Head of SOE Italy). 106.
Stettinius, Harold. 79.
Stott, Captain Donald John (British liaison officer). 11, 91-107, 108.
Stroop, SS Oberführer Jurgen. (Chief of German Police in Athens). 105.
Supplying of Resistance. 36, 55, 111-12, 121-2, 128-9.
Svolos, Professor Alexandros. 45, 46, 47-50, 86.

Talbot-Rice, D. (SOE operative in London). 96.
Tass Agency. 21-2.
Tavoularis, Anastasios (Minister for Interior in Greek Collaborationist Government). 134.
Teheran Conference. 20.
Tito, Marshal. 17, 53, 57, 61, 76, 82, 87, 110.
Trade Unions (Greek). 78, 109.
Tripartite Pact. 16.
Truman Doctrine. 30, 123.
Tsaldaris, Konstantinos (politician of the Right, Prime Minister in 1946). 29.
Tsigantes, General Christos (former Republican officer). 61.
Tsigantes, Major John (Republican officer, brother of above) 33, 103.
Tsipas, Andreas (member of KKE Central Committee). 67.

Tsolakoglou, General George. (first collaborationist Prime Minister). 63-4.
Tsouderos, Emmanouil (Prime Minister of Greek Government in exile). 32, 33, 39, 45-7, 98.
TUC. 85, 87.
Turkey. 16, 95.
Tzimas, Andreas (former KKE member of parliament, EAM representative on ELAS Command; later EAM liaison officer for the Balkans). 67, 76, 98, 114 (under *nom-de-guerre* Vasilis Samariniotis).

United Nations Organisation. 26.

Vafiadis, Markos (ELAS capetan on Macedonia Command, later c-in-c of Democratic Army in 1947-9 Civil War). 115, 119.
Varkiza Agreement. 59, 72, 78-9, 90.
Velouchiotis, Aris (*nom-de-guerre* of Thanasis Klaras, capetan on ELAS Command). 37, 58, 60-1, 109, 120, 132.
Venizelist movement. 39, 114.
Venizelos, Eleftherios (Greek statesman d. 1936). 54.
Venizelos, Sophocles (son of above, Prime Minister in 1944). 44, 45, 46-7, 123.
Voulpiotis, Ioannis (businessman close to collaborationist governments). 105.
Vukmanović-Tempo, General Svetozar. (Tito's representative in Yugoslav Macedonia). 17-18.
Vyshinski, Andrei (Soviet Assistant Foreign Minister). 27.

Walther (German interpreter). 94, 103.
Welke. 103-5.
Wilson of Libya, Field-Marshal Lord. 52, 55, 116.
Woodhouse, Colonel C.M. (Head of British & later Allied Military Mission 1943-4). 21, 34, 37, 38, 39, 56, 71, 93, 97, 103, 104, 108, 109, 111, 120, 131.

Yalta Agreement. 12, 56.
Yugoslavia. 15, 17, 18, 26, 27, 28, 29, 53, 67, 76, 118, 119, 133.
YVE (Right-wing organisation in N. Greece). 114.

Zachariadis, Nikos (Secretary-General of KKE). 29, 75, 77.
Zervas, Colonel Napoleon (Republican officer, later Major-General, commander of EDES). 21, 33, 34, 36-39, 40, 58, 70-1, 108, 109-10, 113, 116, 119, 120, 121, 122, 125, 126, 128, 129, 130, 131, 132.
Zevgos, Yannis (member of KKE Political Bureau, Minister in National Unity Government). 77.